FRANCIS LARKIN, SS. CC.

UNDERSTANDING THE HEART

THE HEART OF JESUS AND SUFFERING

In this month of June, consecrated to the Sacred Heart of Jesus, it is natural and a pleasure for me to exhort you to recall to your minds your hope and your prayer to that Heart "which has loved men so much" and which continues to love us with his twofold love, divine and human, especially those who are more troubled, tearful, and suffering.

From the Heart of Christ, "full of goodness and love", you can obtain strength and comfort in your sufferings, peace in your heart, and merit in all your pains!

> Pope John Paul II, speaking to a group of sick pilgrims, General Audience of June 13, 1979.

THE HEART OF JESUS AND THE FAMILY

Always keep your eyes on the Sacred Heart of Jesus, King and Center of all hearts.

From him you will learn the great lesson of love, of goodness, of sacrifice, of piety, so necessary for every Christian family.

From him you will obtain strength, serenity, authentic and profound happiness for your married life! You will draw down his blessing, if the image of his Heart—besides being impressed on your mind—is always exposed and honored on the wall of your home!

> Pope John Paul II, speaking to newlyweds at the General Audience of June 13, 1979.

Both quotes translated from the Italian edition of *L'Osservatore Romano*, June 15–16, 1979.

UNDERSTANDING THE HEART

by
FRANCIS LARKIN, SS. CC.
National Director
Enthronement of the Sacred Heart

SECOND, REVISED EDITION

IGNATIUS PRESS   SAN FRANCISCO

First edition ©1975
Men of the Sacred Heart
Sacred Heart Center

Cum permissu superiorum
With ecclesiastical approval
© Congregation of the Sacred Hearts 1980
Fairhaven, MA 02719
All rights reserved
ISBN 0-89870-007-8
LC 80-81066
Printed in the United States of America

CONTENTS

	Key to Abbreviations	7
	Introduction	9
	Preface to Revised Edition	13
1.	"Heart" in Everyday Language	15
2.	The Use of "Heart" in Sacred Scripture	
	In the Old Testament	18
	In the New Testament	24
3.	Symbolism of the Heart of Jesus	30
4.	A Sign of Salvation	36
5.	What Is Meant by "Devotion"?	40
6.	Origin of Devotion to the Sacred Heart of Jesus	43
7.	God's Love—Basis of This Devotion	49
8.	God Makes Promises!	52
9.	The Eucharist—Gift of the Heart of Jesus	56
10.	The Heart of Jesus and Reparation	64

11. The Heart of Jesus—Source and
    Symbol of Unity   70
12. The Holy Spirit: Living Water from the
    Pierced Heart of Jesus   75
13. Vatican II and the Heart of Jesus   86
14. The Heart of Jesus and the
    "Domestic Church"   90
15. Sacred Heart Apostolates   97
16. The Heart of Jesus and the Immaculate
    Heart of Mary   101
    Appendix   113

KEY TO ABBREVIATIONS

HA: Pius XII, *Haurietis Aquas*, "On Devotion to the Sacred Heart", an approved revision of the unofficial Vatican Polyglot Press translation, edited by Father Francis Larkin, SS. CC. Milwaukee: International Institute of the Heart of Jesus, 1976.

HS: Stierli, S. J., Rev. Josef, *Heart of the Saviour*. New York: Herder and Herder, 1958.

ESH: Larkin, Rev. Francis, SS. CC., *Enthronement of the Sacred Heart*. Boston, Mass.: St. Paul Editions, 1978.

OFL: Walsh, William Thomas, *Our Lady of Fatima*. New York: Image Books, 1947.

JRH: *Jesus Reveals His Heart: The Letters of St. Margaret Mary*. Boston, Mass.: St. Paul's Editions, 1980.

INTRODUCTION

In common language, "heart" has many meanings.

Here are a few listed in Webster's Collegiate Dictionary: "a muscular organ; the emotional, as distinguished from the intellectual, nature, as 'heart and head often disagree'; courage, spirit; conscience, moral sensibility; temperament, mood; a man, a person; the inmost character; sincerity."

To understand the heart, therefore, is to understand the personality, the character of a man. This is true of the heart of man and it is true of the Heart of the God-Man, Jesus Christ.

Christ had a human Heart, moved by all the human emotions: love, fear, anger, joy, desire, desolation, pity, weakness. Examples of each of these emotions are found in the Gospels.

God permitted the Heart of his Son to be opened on Calvary. St. John signalized this event as something extraordinary and important. This was the beginning of the veneration of the Heart of Jesus that has continued down through the centuries. For over one hundred years, the Catholic Church has sanctioned and encouraged the public liturgical and private cult of the Sacred Heart of Jesus.

Pope Pius XII wrote that "devotion to the Heart of Jesus is the most capable of assisting the present-day needs of the Church and the human race."

Pope Paul VI has stated that "the Heart of Christ is the primary source of the liturgy." Speaking to the Jesuits he affirmed: "The cult rendered to the Sacred Heart is the most efficacious means to contribute to that spiritual and moral renewal of the world called for by the Second Vatican Council."

To grasp the full import of these strong statements about the Heart of Jesus, we must understand the meaning of the word "heart" as used in the language of men of all cultures and races from time immemorial.

Dietrich von Hildebrand, the eminent philosopher and author, puts this very clearly:

> The role that the Church grants to the devotion to the Sacred Heart and the increasing emphasis laid on this aspect of the mystery of the Incarnation, carries with it a great challenge—namely, that we

deepen our understanding of the heart as one of the fundamental centers of man's soul. . . . We cannot understand the devotion to the Sacred Heart in its true meaning, or in its specific mission to melt our hearts, unless we first discover the true nature of the heart and the grandeur and glory of true affectivity.[1]

In a recent article on moral questions arising from heart transplants, it is stated that "scarcely any other organ in the human body is touched and formed by the whole personality, by its passions and desires, its experiences, virtues and vices as is a man's heart, and physicians attribute many heart ailments to unresolved psychic problems. It is not only in common thought and speech and in that of poets that the heart is considered a symbol of the whole person. Psychoanalytical and psychosomatic sciences show that there is often a close link between psychical states and neurotic heart disorders."[2]

The Old Testament abounds in the use of the word "heart". The same is true of the New Testament. All this was a preparation by the Holy Spirit for the great revelation of the love of the

---

[1] *The Sacred Heart* (Baltimore-Dublin: Helicon Press, 1965).

[2] The Apostleship of Prayer Director's Service, Rome (August-September, 1968).

Heart of hearts, the Heart of Christ, the God-Man; a Heart whose love was manifested by his words and deeds in Palestine; a Heart opened on Calvary; a Heart presented to the human race at Paray-le-Monial—a flaming Heart to save a world aflame.

Only God can change and heal the heart which he created and the depths and feelings of which he alone knows. "And I will take away the stony heart and will give them a heart of flesh" (Ezek 11:19). Our blessed Savior began his public career by saying he had come to heal the brokenhearted: "The Spirit of the Lord is upon me . . . to heal the broken-hearted" (Lk 4:18. See Is 61:1).

The merciful Heart of Jesus, opened on Calvary in his very sacrificial act, is still open to all who will turn to it with trust and who are ready to open their hearts to receive his Spirit of healing love.

Francis Larkin, SS. CC.

AUTHOR'S PREFACE
TO THE REVISED EDITION

Two chapters have been added: Chapter 10, "The Heart of Jesus and Reparation", and Chapter 12, "The Holy Spirit: Living Water from the Pierced Heart of Jesus".

Many Catholics are discovering "a treasure hidden in a field" (Mt 13:44)—the wounded Heart of Jesus, hidden in his Body, but brought to light through the inspiration of his Holy Spirit. Further, they have discovered another treasure—a "pearl of great price"—namely, that the Holy Spirit is a gift of the Heart of Jesus, a gift promised on the Feast of the Tabernacles (Jn 7:37) and fulfilled on Good Friday, when Jesus' Heart was opened by a soldier's lance and blood and water came out (Jn 19:34).

While the discovery of this hidden treasure may be a recent one for Christians of today, this treasure was already known from the beginnings of Christianity, as readers of this modest book will learn.

I like to think that today we are witnessing the verification of the words of St. John: "There are three that bear witness: the Spirit and the water and the blood; and these three are one" (1 Jn 5:8). They are witnessing to the existential reality of the Pierced Heart of Jesus, the source and symbol of the infinite, merciful Love—life-giving water—the Lord is pouring out on mankind from heaven and from the Eucharist.

"Let him who thirsts come; and who wishes, let him receive the water of life freely" (Rev 22:17).

I am grateful to friends for several suggested corrections and changes which have improved the text and to Ignatius Press for the publication of this second edition.

Francis Larkin, SS. CC.

CHAPTER 1

"HEART" IN EVERYDAY LANGUAGE

1. Give some common examples of the use of the word "heart".

"Have a heart . . . he is all heart . . . put your heart into your work." People are called: "hard-hearted, tender-hearted, big-hearted, warm-hearted, cold-hearted, chicken-hearted, heartless."

2. In what sense is the word "heart" used here?

In a symbolic sense as describing the emotions, affections—or lack of them—attitudes, feelings.

3. What is a symbol?

"That which suggests something else by reason of relationship, association, convention; especially a visible sign of something invisible" (Webster).

4. Is the heart considered a symbol of the person?

Yes, as in "stout hearts that follow me", "I give you my heart."

5. In what category does Father Karl Rahner place the word "heart"?

As a primal word, falling into the category of words used for the whole man, such as "head", "hand" (cf. HS 132).

6. Does it have this primal character in other cultures besides our Western culture?

Yes, it is so used in Semitic, Greco-Roman, Mexican, Egyptian, Indian, and Mohammedan cultures.

7. Is the physical heart of man used as a symbol of his personal "center"—as the origin and kernel of everything else in the human person?

"'Heart' is an image common to all mankind for the central point of a personality, the basis on which his whole being is built up, and from which flows everything that he is and does. The 'heart', therefore, signifies both the essence of the person as he actually is, and also the origin of his actions, his fundamental existential attitude. It signifies a person's disposition: the way he looks at other people, at life and at all that exists. According to this image, the merciful person opens his heart, the innermost center of his personality, to the misery and suffering of another, and is so consistent in this existential generosity that it becomes a permanent disposition."[1]

8. Is the heart always a symbol of love?

No, for the heart can be said to be "love-less" or "evil". Our Lord himself tells us, "From the heart of men come evil thoughts" (Mk 7:21). Even though the heart is a *common* symbol of love, it is fully and completely so only in the case of Our Lord. As Father Rahner says, "To find that the innermost core, the ultimate reality of a person is love, is something we experience only in the Heart of Our Lord" (HS 133).

9. Why is this?

Because Jesus is God and "God is love" (1 Jn 4:16). As someone has said, "He is all heart!"

[1] Ladislaus Boros, S. J., *God Is With Us* (New York: Herder and Herder, 1967) 50–51.

CHAPTER 2

THE USE OF "HEART" IN SACRED SCRIPTURE

IN THE OLD TESTAMENT

10. How important is the understanding of the biblical use of "heart"?

"The criterion of genuine devotion to the Sacred Heart is the degree to which its biblical basis is appreciated" (H. Rahner, HS 35).

Of course this does not mean that only those who are familiar with Scripture have a genuine devotion to the Sacred Heart. Many persons devoted to the Heart of Jesus do not always understand its biblical basis, nor do all those versed in Scripture understand devotion to the Sacred Heart: "I bless you, Father, Lord of heaven and of earth, for hiding these things from the learned and the clever and revealing them to mere children" (Mt 11:25).

11. What did Pope Pius XII write on this point?

"We are absolutely convinced that not until we have made a profound study of the primary and loftier nature of this devotion, with the aid of the light of the divinely revealed truth, can we rightly and fully appreciate its incomparable excellence and the inexhaustible abundance of its heavenly favors" (HA no. 19).

12. Is "heart" the type of word capable of being used in a world religion?

Yes, because it is a primal word used in so many world cultures.

13. Is this true of the Judaeo-Christian religion?

So much so that Fr. Hugo Rahner calls it "That fundamental word so beloved of the Holy Spirit" (HS 29).

14. What else did Father Rahner say of heart in Scripture?

"In the language of revelation, the hallowed word 'heart' and its almost synonymous equivalents (Hebrew: *leb, lebab, beten, kereb*; Greek: *kardia, koilia, splanchna*; Latin: *cor, venter, viscera*) have the same primal meaning as in all human language" (HS 17).

15. How is "heart" used in the Old Testament?

"The connotation of 'heart' in the Old Testament has been well summarized in a recent work: 'Heart' is the principle and organ of the personal life of man, the center in which the being and activity of man as a spiritual personality are concentrated, and consequently the source and center of his religious and ethical life" (H. Rahner, HS 17).

16. Can you give some examples?

Here are a few (there are literally hundreds): "Why do you harden your hearts as Egypt and Pharaoh did?" (1 Sam 6:6) "Let your hearts be broken, not your garments torn" (Joel 2:13). "You shall love the Lord your God with all your heart. . . . Let these words . . . be written on your heart" (Dt 6:5). "I will place my Law within them and write it upon their hearts" (Jer 31:33).

17. Are there any texts in which God uses "heart" as applied to himself?

"I shall choose a faithful priest who shall do what I have in my heart and mind" (1 Sam 2:35).

"I will give you shepherds after my own heart. . . " (Jer 3:15). "Yahweh regretted having made man . . . and his heart grieved" (Gen 6:6). "I will replant them firmly in this land, with all my heart and soul" (Jer 32:41).

18. Is the word "heart" frequently used in the Psalms?

In almost every Psalm, 113 times to be exact. Some examples: "You put gladness into my heart" (4:8). ". . .exult, all you upright of heart" (32:11). ". . .with all my heart I will observe your precepts" (119:69). "Take delight in the Lord, and he will grant you your heart's request" (37:4). "My heart had been smoldering inside me" (39:3).

19. Are there any explicit references to the Heart of the Messiah in the Messianic prophecies?

Yes, and they are most important. "Here we are careful to discuss only those Messianic texts of the Old Testament whose reference to Jesus is guaranteed by the witness of the New. What we wish to prove is that God really intended the revelation of the Heart of the Messiah, and that this revelation belongs to the original message and meaning of inspired Scripture" (H. Rahner, HS 22).

20. What are these texts?

"To do your will, O my God, is my delight, and your law is within my heart!" (Ps 40; see also, Heb 10:5–7). "Their prince shall be one of their own . . . he can come close to me; who else, indeed, would risk his life?" (Jer 30:21)

21. What is the significance of these two texts?

The first, from Psalm 40, is a Messianic prayer which epitomizes all that passed in the Heart of Jesus of Nazareth: surrender to the will of the Father who sent him, even to the surrender of his dead body in the sacrifice of atonement. In the second, "he can come close to me" is to be understood as the movement of a priest towards the altar in answer to God's invitation. In this office of sacrifice, he must give his heart in pledge, he must plight his life in order to buy and ensure the treasures of salvation for all men. Jesus in very truth gave his Heart in pledge when he drew near to God for the priestly office of sacrifice at the Last Supper and on Calvary (HS 23–24).

22. Is there another text from Jeremiah?

". . .the anger of God will not turn aside until he has . . . carried out the decision of his heart" (Jer 30:24).

23. What is the meaning of this Messianic prophecy?

Here "the prophetic vision of Jeremiah reaches beyond this pledged heart to the Day of Judgment. It sees the disregarded love of the Redeemer's Heart changed into the majestic anger of God which breaks forth from the Messiah and brings 'the plans of his heart' to eternal realization" (HS 24).

24. Are there any references to the Heart of Christ in the Messianic Psalms?

"My heart is like wax, melting inside me" (22:15). "Insults have broken my heart" (69:20). "So my heart exults, my very soul rejoices . . . you will not abandon my soul. . . ." (16:9)

25. Explain these texts.

The first two refer to the sufferings of the Messiah. The third refers to the joys of the Messiah at his Resurrection. St. Peter quoted this passage in his first sermon (Acts 2:25–28).

26. What picture emerges from all these mysterious prophecies?

"One sublime picture of the innermost dispositions of the future Messiah; and the element that fuses them is that fundamental word so beloved of the Holy Spirit: the Heart. The Heart of the Lord's Anointed is submissive to the God who sent him; it is humble and self-sacrificing. It is a Heart full of majestic anger, or sunk in mortal anguish, or leaping with ecstatic joy" (H. Rahner, HS 29).

27. Is there another "heart" text in the Psalms?

Yes, the one used in the entrance hymn for the solemnity of the Sacred Heart: "But the plan of the Lord stands forever; the design of his heart, through all generations. . . . He who fashioned the heart of each . . . in him our hearts rejoice. . . ." (33:11, 15, 21)

IN THE NEW TESTAMENT

28. What about the Gospels—did Christ use the word "heart" in his preaching?

Yes, many times: "For a man's words flow out of what fills his heart" (Mt 12:34). "Why do you have such wicked thoughts in your hearts?" (Mt 9:4) "Wherever your treasure lies, there your heart will be" (Lk 12:34). "Happy the pure in heart" (Mt 5:8). "You foolish men, so slow [of heart] to believe" (Lk 24:25).

29. What effect on men's hearts did Jesus' words have?

"And they said to one another, 'Were not our hearts burning inside us as he talked to us on the road. . . ?' " (Lk 24:32)

30. Did Christ speak of his own Heart in the Gospels?

Yes. "My heart is moved with pity for the crowd" (Mt 15:32). "Come to me, all you who are weary . . . I will refresh you . . . for I am gentle and humble of heart" (Mt 11:28–29). "If anyone thirsts, let him come to me and drink. He who believes in me, as the Scripture has said: 'Out of his heart shall flow rivers of living waters.' Now this he said about the Spirit, which those who believed in him were to receive" (Jn 7:37).

31. When was this prophecy fulfilled?

When Longinus opened Jesus' side with his spear and "immediately blood and water flowed out" (Jn 19:34), symbols of the outpouring of the Holy Spirit and the birth of the Church, for "The Church was born from the wounded Heart of the Redeemer."[1]

The reason for this statement is this: Water symbolizes baptism; blood, the Eucharist. These are the two basic, constitutive sacraments of the Church (see below, Chap. 11, Q 124). On this point Pope Pius XII wrote: "Under the influence of this love, our Savior, by the outpouring of his Blood, became wedded to his Church.... Hence, from the wounded Heart of the Redeemer was born the Church, the dispenser of the Blood of the Redemption...." (HA no. 76)

32. What may we conclude from all these biblical texts?

That the heart is "the focal point of man's primal integral relations with others and above all with God; for God is concerned with the whole man, and in his divine actions it is to man's center, his heart, that he addresses his graces and his judgments" (K. Rahner, HS 133).

33. Are there other scriptural texts to illustrate this statement?

[1] Pope Paul VI, *Diserti Interpretes Facti* (May 25, 1965).

Here are some from St. Paul: "God has sent the Spirit of his Son into our hearts" (Gal 4:6). "By believing from the heart you are made righteous" (Rom 10:10). "You stubborn people with your pagan hearts" (Acts 7:51). "You have a permanent place in my heart" (Phil 1:7).

34. Did St. Paul ever refer to the Heart of Jesus?

Yes, in his letter to the Philippians: "I long for you all in the heart of Christ" (Phil 1:8).

35. What is the mutual relationship between the Gospels and the Heart of Jesus?

Our Lord's wounded and glorified Heart is like a powerful light focusing on and illuminating the merciful and redeeming love of the Savior, the motivation of all his words and deeds.

36. What did St. Gregory the Great write in this regard?

"Learn the Heart of God in the words of God, that you may long more ardently for things eternal" (cited in HA no. 65).

37. Are there any further considerations on the importance of a scriptural understanding of devotion to the Heart of Jesus?

"The sense in which the phrase 'Heart of Our Lord' has been understood from the earliest times in the prayers of the Church and of her devout children is precisely that of Holy Scripture. . . . Every failure to understand the eternal word 'heart' is a real tragedy of the spirit. And, on the other hand, whenever men learn the secrets of the Heart of Our Lord Jesus Christ with a knowledge which is authentic (in other words, founded on Scripture) and interior, there something decisive has taken place in the realm of the spirit: God has been understood in the way in which he offered himself for understanding—from heart to heart" (H. Rahner, HS 18–19).

38. May we conclude from all this that devotion to the Heart of Jesus did not begin with the revelations at Paray-le-Monial?

Yes. We can trace the origins of the devotion back to Scripture, and specifically to Calvary when Our Lord's Heart was opened. With the writings of the Fathers of the Church there begins an unbroken tradition of thought and writing stretching down through the centuries. One example suffices. In Justin Martyr (2nd c.) we read: "We Christians are the true Israel which springs from Christ; for we are carved out of his

Heart (*koilia*) as from a rock. . . . He makes living water overflow into the hearts of those who through him love the Father of the universe, and he satiates those who drink the water of life" (*Dialogue* 144, 4; cited in HS 45).

At Paray-le-Monial, Jesus requested the establishment of an official, liturgical feast in honor of his Heart, to be celebrated in the universal Church. Even though this request was not implemented until 1856, it is safe to say the present *liturgical* cult of the Heart of Jesus had its origin in the revelations at Paray. Here is what Father Karl Rahner writes on this point:

"Theology can and must show that the devotion to the Sacred Heart is materially contained in Scripture and in patristic and medieval tradition . . . nevertheless this abstract dogmatic argument and the indication of a precedent will not provide sufficient basis for the present devotion to the Sacred Heart. For this we must appeal to the 'private revelations' of Paray-le-Monial, or, if you wish, to the Church's acceptance (historically occasioned by the revelations) of the present devotion, which certainly did not always exist in its present form" (HS 139).

CHAPTER 3

SYMBOLISM OF THE SACRED HEART OF JESUS

39. What did Pope Pius XII write about the image and symbolism of the physical Heart of Jesus in Haurietis Aquas?

He called it the "image which surpasses all the rest in efficacy and meaning, namely, the pierced Heart of the crucified Christ" (HA no. 103). Again: "The clearest image of this all-embracing fullness of God is the Heart of Christ Jesus itself. We mean the fullness of mercy...." (no. 100) Here are some other texts: "Nothing therefore prevents our adoring the Sacred Heart of Jesus Christ as having a part in and being the natural and expressive symbol of the abiding love with which the divine Redeemer is still on fire for mankind" (no. 85). "And so the Heart of our Savior reflects in some way the image of the divine Person of the Word and, at the same time, of his twofold nature, the human and the divine; in it we can consider not only the symbol but, in a sense, the summary of the whole mystery of our redemption" (no. 86). "In this special manifestation [to St. Margaret Mary] Christ pointed to his Heart, with definite and repeated words, as the symbol by which men should be attracted to a knowledge and recognition of his love; and at the same time he established it as a sign or pledge of mercy and grace for the needs of the Church of our times" (no. 97).

40. What is the threefold symbolism of Our Lord's Heart?

Pius XII answers: It is "the chief sign and symbol of that threefold love with which the divine Redeemer unceasingly loves his Eternal Father and all mankind." First, "of that *divine love* which he shares with the Father and the Holy Spirit. . . ." Second, it is the "symbol of that *burning love which, infused into his soul*, enriches the human will of Christ. . . ." Third, "it is the symbol also of *sensible* love. . . ." [that is, of his emotional affections] (no. 54–56).

41. When we look upon an image of the Heart of Jesus, of what should we be reminded?

Of love—of the love of Jesus for his Father and of his merciful love for men. The Heart of

Jesus has been called a "digest" of the greatest story ever told, the story of his eternal love for sinful mankind.

42. When we honor a Sacred Heart image, what do we honor?

We honor the reality behind the symbol—the Person of Jesus, who is a God of love. In like manner, when we honor the flag, we show respect for our country "for which it stands".

43. Did Our Lord ask us to venerate and pay honor to his Heart?

Yes, when he appeared to St. Margaret Mary in the 17th century. Here is what she writes: "Our divine Lord assured me that he takes a singular pleasure in being honored under the figure of his physical Heart. He wishes the image of this Heart to be exposed in public and honored" (JRH 35, 8, 36, 131, 133).

44. How did Our Lord show his Heart?

St. Margaret Mary describes the vision of 1674:
"After that I saw this divine Heart as on a throne of flames, more brilliant than the sun and

transparent as crystal. It had its adorable wound and was encircled with a crown of thorns, which signified the hurts our sins caused him. It was surmounted by a cross which signified that, from the first moment of his Incarnation, that is, from the time this Sacred Heart was formed, the cross was planted in it; that it was filled, from the very first moment, with all the bitterness, humiliations, poverty, sorrow, and contempt his sacred humanity would have to suffer during the whole course of his life and during his holy Passion" (JRH 133).

45. Why did Our Lord ask that his Heart be so honored?

One reason he gave was that his Heart might receive as much love and honor as it had received insult and humiliation during his Passion. But even more significant, it was part of his plan for "renewing the effects of his redemption". St. Margaret Mary explains this plan: "He made me understand that the ardent desire he had of being loved by men and of drawing them from the path of perdition into which Satan was hurrying them in great numbers, had caused him to fix upon this plan of manifesting his Heart to men, together with all its treasures of love, mercy, grace, sanctification and salvation" (JRH 133).

46. What did our Savior promise to those who publicly honored his Heart?

"Wherever this sacred image would be exposed for veneration, he would pour forth his graces and blessings...." (JRH 133) "He promised he would pour out in abundance into the hearts of all those who honor his Heart all the gifts with which it is filled, and that everywhere this image is exposed and honored, it would draw down all kinds of blessings" (ESH 48).

47. Did he promise to bless families that honor his Heart?

Yes, many times. For instance: "Since he is the source of all blessings, he will shower them in abundance on every place where an image of his divine Heart is honored. He will reunite broken families, will protect and help those in necessity and those who approach him in confidence" (JRH 36, 131).

48. Does the Church encourage the public and private veneration of the image of the Sacred Heart?

Very much so. "Thus it is absolutely necessary that the faithful venerate and honor this Heart, in the expression of their private piety as well as in the services of public cult. . . ."[1]

49. Does the Church permit the use of the image of the Heart of Jesus alone?

For private devotion, yes. Examples would be: the Sacred Heart badge, banners, pictures, symbols, for non-liturgical use. *For liturgical use*, that is, "exposed for public veneration on altars," no.[2]

[1] Pope Paul VI, *Diserti Interpretes Facti* (May 25, 1965). Cf. Appendix, *Haurietis Aquas*, 56.

[2] Decree of Congregation of Rites, August 26, 1891.

CHAPTER 4

A SIGN OF SALVATION

50. What is the relevance of the Heart of Jesus to salvation?

Pope Pius XII in *Haurietis Aquas* wrote: "Behold, today, another true sign of God's favor is presented to our gaze, namely, the Sacred Heart of Jesus. . . . In it must all our hopes be placed; *from it salvation is to be sought and hoped for*" (HA no. 121).

51. What was the "other true sign" to which the Pope referred?

In this passage the Holy Father was quoting from the Sacred Heart Encyclical *Annum Sacrum* of Leo XIII, issued in 1899. Pope Leo recalled the appearance of a cross in the sky to the Emperor Constantine as a pledge of the victory to follow. Here is the passage: "When the Church in the days immediately succeeding her institution, was oppressed beneath the yoke of the Caesars, a young emperor saw in the heavens a cross, which became at once the happy omen and cause of the glorious victory that soon followed. And now today, behold another blessed and heavenly token is offered to our sight—the most Sacred Heart of Jesus, with a cross rising from it and shining forth with dazzling splendor amidst flames of love. In that Sacred Heart all our hopes should be placed, and from it the salvation of men is to be confidently sought."[1]

52. What was the occasion of this encyclical of Leo XIII?

The consecration of the human race to the Heart of Jesus in 1899. Pope Leo called this act "the greatest act of my pontificate".

53. Did Pope Pius XI repeat the words of Leo XIII that in the Sacred Heart is to be found our only hope of salvation?

Yes, in his encyclical "On Reparation Due to the Sacred Heart."[2] Pope Pius IX had said the same thing over a century ago.

[1] In *The Great Encyclicals of Pope Leo XIII* (New York: Benziger Brothers, 1903).

[2] National Catholic Welfare Conference [now, United States Catholic Conference], Washington, D. C. (1928).

54. What did Pius XII say about the practice of devotion to the Sacred Heart of Jesus?

"It is likewise Our most fervent desire that all who profess themselves Christians and are seriously engaged in the effort to establish the kingdom of Christ on earth will consider the practice of devotion to the Heart of Jesus as the *source and symbol of unity, salvation and peace*" (HA no. 122).

55. Do we find in the writings of St. Margaret Mary specific references to devotion to the Sacred Heart as a means of salvation?

Yes. "He wants to establish his reign among us anew only to impart more abundantly his graces of sanctification and salvation" (JRH 97).

56. Are there any other references in her writings?

Many more—here are a few: "[Devotion to the Sacred Heart] is as a last effort of the Savior to draw sinners to repentance and to give them abundantly efficacious and sanctifying graces to work out their salvation. . . ." (JRH 102) "I am convinced . . . there is no surer way to salvation than to consecrate oneself to this divine Heart" (JRH 58). "This devotion was as a last effort of his love which wished to favor men in these last centuries with this loving redemption, in order to withdraw them from the empire of Satan, which he intended to destroy, and in order to put us under the sweet liberty of the empire of his love. This he would establish in the hearts of all those who would embrace this devotion" (JRH 133).

57. What, in your opinion, is the reason we are to look for salvation from the practice of devotion to the Sacred Heart of Jesus?

For these reasons, it seems to me: 1) Our Lord has promised it; 2) since the practice of this devotion increases personal love for God and neighbor, by fulfilling these commandments we will be saved; 3) devotion to the Sacred Heart (according to Our Lord's plan) leads to a greater participation in the Eucharist, the pledge of our salvation.

CHAPTER 5

WHAT IS MEANT BY "DEVOTION"?

58. What do we mean by "devotion"?

St. Thomas defines devotion as: "A willingness to give oneself readily to what concerns the service of God" (quoted in HA no. 109).

59. Apply this to the devotion to the Sacred Heart of Jesus.

This is a service of God dedicated to love—"service which pays homage to the divine love and is offered for the sake of that love" (HA no. 109).

60. How did Pope Pius XII define devotion to the Sacred Heart?

"Devotion to the Sacred Heart of Jesus, of its very nature, is a worship of the love with which God, through Jesus, loved us, and at the same time, an exercise of our own love by which we are related to God and to other men" (HA no. 107).

61. Does, then, devotion to the Heart of Jesus include and foster practical love for one's fellow man?

Yes. "Devotion of this kind is directed towards the love of God for us, in order to adore it, give thanks for it, and live so as to imitate it; it has this in view, as the end to be attained, that we bring that love by which we are bound to God and to the rest of men to perfect fulfillment by carrying out daily more eagerly the New Commandment . . . 'that you love one another as I have loved you' " (HA no. 107).

62. Can you give some examples of this outgoing love among great lovers and apostles of the Sacred Heart of Jesus?

Yes, just to mention a few: *St. Margaret Mary*, who helped to establish the first hospital at Paray-le-Monial, which still exists; *Blessed Claude Colombière*, S. J., St. Margaret Mary's spiritual director, who sacrificed his life serving English Catholics during the penal days; *Blessed Mary of the Divine Heart*, a former German countess, who was the instrument of God in the consecration of the human race to the Sacred Heart in 1899. She died in great sufferings while serving wayward girls in Oporto, Portugal. *Father Charles de Foucauld*, founder of the Little Brothers and Sisters of Jesus, who was killed while witnessing Christ in the Sahara; *Father Damien de Veuster, SS. CC.* , "Apostle of the Lepers", a great lover of the Sacred Heart in the Blessed Sacrament; *Father Mateo Crawley-Boevey, SS. CC.* , "Apostle of the Sacred Heart", who spent himself for fifty years preaching the merciful love of the Sacred Heart all over the world; *all the Popes* since Pius IX, but especially *Pope John XXIII*, a great lover of the Sacred Heart, who was the "Apostle of the Second Commandment".

63. *What, then, is another word for Devotion?*

Devotedness—to the love of God and love of neighbor; devotedness to the Heart of Jesus in the Eucharist and to Christ in one's fellow man; devotedness to the Church, to the Holy Father, to one's family, to duty, to country. This is what we mean by saying a person is "*devoted* to the Heart of Jesus".

CHAPTER 6

ORIGIN OF DEVOTION TO THE SACRED HEART OF JESUS

64. When did devotion to the Sacred Heart really begin?

To answer this question properly, we must make a distinction between the liturgical practice of this devotion, as it is approved by the Church, and the doctrinal basis of the practices of the devotion.

65. When did the former begin?

At the time Christ, in a private revelation, requested the establishment of liturgical practices in honor of his divine Heart in the Church.

66. When and where did this take place?

Between 1673 and 1675, at Paray-le-Monial in France, where Our Lord appeared a number of times to St. Margaret Mary, a Visitation nun.

67. What did the Church say about these private revelations at Paray?

By canonizing Margaret Mary the Church approved her writings, which contained detailed accounts of the revelations.

68. What can be concluded from this?

These revelations contain nothing against faith and morals.

69. Does this approval mean that these revelations are necessarily authentic or that Our Lord really made them to the saint?

No. Yet if we have no absolute certainty, we possess at least reliable guarantees which justify our believing in the reality and genuineness of these revelations, without incurring the reproach of incredulity and imprudence.

70. What are some of these "reliable guarantees"?

The attitude of the Church with reference to them: Popes Pius IX, Leo XIII, St. Pius X, Benedict XV, Pius XI, Pius XIII, John XXIII, and Paul VI have cited them in official documents, including encyclicals, as realities worthy of our adhesion.

71. In what encyclicals were these revelations referred to?

Annum Sacrum of Leo XIII, On the Consecration of the Human Race to the Sacred Heart (1899), *Miserentissimus Redemptor* of Pius XI, On Reparation Due to the Sacred Heart (1928), *Haurietis Aquas* of Pius XII, On the Nature of True Devotion to the Heart of Jesus (1956).

72. What, then, should be our attitude towards these revelations?

1) We may believe in them without any fear of being mistaken; 2) one would behave imprudently and even rashly in opposing one's own judgment to that of the Church; 3) we should be humble and grateful that Our Lord in his great mercy would deign to give us poor sinners such a further great proof of his concern for us and such a simple but powerful means for our sanctification and salvation.

73. Why may we have such certitude towards these revelations?

Because in the matter of private revelations the Church never proceeds incautiously. Moreover, although the Church does not pledge her infallibility in these matters, she is nevertheless, as we know, an absolutely reliable guide even as regards the piety of the faithful.

74. What did Pope Pius XII say in Haurietis Aquas *about minimizing the importance of devotion to the Sacred Heart of Jesus?*

"There is no question here of some ordinary form of piety which anyone at his own whim may treat as of little consequence or set aside as inferior to others. . . . Consequently, to consider of little worth this signal benefit conferred on the Church by Jesus Christ would be to do something both rash and harmful and also deserving of God's displeasure" (HA no. 109–110).

75. What does Father Karl Rahner, S. J. , have to say on the private revelations made at Paray?

"Theology can and must show that the devotion to the Sacred Heart is materially contained in Scripture and in patristic and medieval tradition. Nevertheless, this abstract dogmatic argument and the indication of a precedent will not provide sufficient basis for the present devotion to the Sacred Heart. For this we must appeal to the 'private revelations' of Paray-le-Monial, or, if you wish, to the Church's acceptance (historically occasioned by the revelations) of the present devotion, which certainly did not always exist in its present form" (HS 139).

76. What are some of the Church-approved forms of the devotion which did not exist before?

1) *The liturgical cult* of the Sacred Heart: Solemnity of the Sacred Heart, Office of the Sacred Heart, Litany of the Sacred Heart, Consecration to the Sacred Heart of Jesus on the Feast of Christ the King; 2) *Practices of reparation*: Mass of reparation, Communions of reparation, Holy Hours, act of reparation on the Feast of the Sacred Heart; 3) *Enthronement and veneration* of the image of the Sacred Heart; 4) *Consecration* of individuals, families, institutions, and nations to the Sacred Heart.

77. What about the beginning of devotion to the Sacred Heart from a doctrinal standpoint as mentioned in the first question?

With Pope Pius XII, in *Haurietis Aquas*, we can say this devotion had its roots in the Old Testament, was developed in the New Testament, and gradually began to manifest itself in the early centuries of Christianity. In the Middle Ages it was flourishing, especially in monasteries (HA no. 20–61, 94, 95).

78. What is the "doctrine" of the Sacred Heart which had its roots in the Old Testament?

It is the doctrine of love, of merciful love: "God is love" (1 Jn 4:16). Pope Pius XII stated that the divine love for us is the principal object of this devotion, and this love "is proclaimed and insisted upon in the Old and New Testament by the kind of images which strongly arouse our emotions. Since these images were presented in the Sacred Writings foretelling the coming of the Son of God made man, they can be considered as a token of the noblest symbol and witness of that divine love, that is, of the most Sacred and Adorable Heart of the divine Redeemer" (HA no. 23).

79. What, then, is a good doctrinal definition of this devotion?

Pope Pius XII tells us: "This devotion, summarily expressed, is nothing else than devotion [read: 'devotedness'] to the divine and human love of the Incarnate Word and to the love by which the heavenly Father and the Holy Spirit exercise their care over sinful men" (HA no. 89).

CHAPTER 7

GOD'S LOVE—BASIS OF THIS DEVOTION

80. What are some of the Scripture texts from the Old Testament dealing with God's love for the chosen people?

"I have loved you with an everlasting love, [and] I am constant in my affection for you" (Jer 31:3). "See, the days are coming—it is Yahweh who speaks—when I will make a new covenant with the House of Israel. . . . This is the covenant I will make with the House of Israel when those days arrive—it is Yahweh who speaks. Deep within them I will plant my Law, writing it on their hearts. Then I will be their God and they shall be my people" (Jer 31:31–33).

81. What images did God use to describe his unwavering love for men?

"Does a woman forget her baby at the breast, or fail to cherish the son of her womb?" (Is

49:15) A loving covenant written right in the hearts of chosen people (Jer 31:33). The marital love expressed in the Song of Songs.

82. How did Pope Pius XII describe love in the mystery of the redemption?

"The mystery of the divine redemption is primarily and by its very nature a mystery of love, that is, of the perfect love of Christ for his heavenly Father to whom the sacrifice of the Cross, offered in a spirit of love and obedience, presents the most abundant and infinite satisfaction due for the sins of the human race. . . . It is also a mystery of the love of the Most Holy Trinity and of the divine Redeemer towards all men" (HA no. 35, 36).

83. Since love is the motivation of the Incarnation, may we say that the Heart of Jesus is a summary *of our redemption?*

Yes. This is the thought of Pope Pius XII: "And so the Heart of our Savior reflects in some way the image of the divine Person of the Word and, at the same time, of his twofold nature, the human and the divine; in it we can consider not only the symbol, but, in a sense, the summary of the whole mystery of our redemption. When we adore the Sacred Heart of Jesus Christ, we adore in it and through it both the uncreated love of the Divine Word and also its human love and its other emotions and virtues, since both loves moved our Redeemer to sacrifice himself for us and for his Spouse, the Universal Church, as the Apostle declares: 'Christ loved the Church, and delivered himself up for it. . . .' (Eph 5:25–27)" (HA no. 86)

CHAPTER 8

GOD MAKES PROMISES!

84. Is there anything unusual about God making promises to men?

No, the Scriptures are filled with examples.

85. Can you give some?

In the *Old Testament*: The promise of a redeemer (Gen 3:15); promises to Noah (Gen 8:21; 9:7–17); to Abraham (Gen 12:14–17); to Jeremiah (31); to David (2 Sam 17:5–16); and many more.

In the *New Testament*: The promise to Mary (Lk 1:31–37); the Beatitudes (Mt 5:3–12); promise of eternal life through the Eucharist (Jn 6:35–58); promise of the Holy Spirit (Jn 7:37–39; 14:26); to Peter and the Church (Mt 16:18–19).

86. Are these unconditional promises?

Yes, for some; no, for others. *Unconditional*

Promises: The promise of a Redeemer, of the Holy Spirit, of the primacy of Peter, of the indestructibility of the Church. *Conditional Promises*: of eternal life to those who "eat my flesh and drink my blood" (Jn 6:54); of salvation to those who believe, who are baptized and keep the commandments; of those who "seek first the Kingdom of God. . . ." (Mt 6:33)

87. *What about the promises made by Our Lord to St. Margaret Mary? May we safely believe them?*

Yes, for these reasons: 1) They have been approved and cited by the Church; 2) they have been fulfilled many times in the lives of all kinds of people; 3) they are nothing else but an elaboration on the promises of Christ found in the Gospels. Father Karl Rahner writes: "Taken in their entirety, these promises affirm and offer no more than Our Lord himself promised in the Gospel to absolute faith (Mt 17:20; 21:21); (Mk 16:17); (Jn 14:12). What is new in these promises is therefore not their content, but the circumstances of their fulfillment, the fact that what has already been promised in substance in the Gospels is now attached precisely to devotion to the Sacred Heart" (HS 155).

88. Are these unconditional promises?

No. Their fulfillment depends upon our carrying out with faith the requests of Our Lord to which the promises are attached.

89. Can you give examples?

"Since he is the source of all blessings, he will shower them on every place where an image of his Sacred Heart shall be honored, because his love urges him to dispense the inexhaustible treasures of his sanctifying and salutary graces *to all souls of good will. He is looking for empty hearts devoid of self-love* to fill with the sweet unction of his ardent charity, to consume them and transform them into himself. *He is seeking humble and submissive souls that want nothing but the accomplishment of his good pleasure.* Moreover, by this means he will restore broken families and protect those that are in any difficulties" (JRH 131, emphasis added).

90. What is the purpose of these promises?

"If Christ has solemnly promised them in private revelations it was for the purpose of encouraging men to perform with greater fervor the chief duties of the Catholic religion, namely, love and expiation, and thus take all possible measures for their own spiritual advantage" (HA no. 112).

91. To what categories of persons are those promises addressed?

To every class: sinners and those with all kinds of problems; the fervent and lukewarm; Christians and non-Christians; families, religious communities; nations; the dying; priests and all apostles of the devotion; the souls in purgatory.

92. Where are these promises to be found?

In the writings of St. Margaret Mary: in her autobiography, but especially in her *Letters*.

93. Is there a detailed listing of these promises?

Yes, in the book, *Enthronement of the Sacred Heart*, 71 ff.

94. Where can I obtain a new factual, theological and pastoral study of the promises?

In the booklet, *The Promises of Our Lord to St. Margaret Mary*,[1] by Father Paul Wenisch, S. J.

[1] International Institute of the Heart of Jesus, 7700 West Blue Mound Road, Milwaukee, Wisconsin 53201.

CHAPTER 9

THE EUCHARIST—GIFT OF THE HEART OF JESUS

95. Is there an essential relationship between devotion to the Sacred Heart of Jesus and the Eucharist?

According to Pope Paul VI, the essence of devotion to the Sacred Heart of Jesus is adoring and making reparation to Christ Jesus especially in the most sacred mystery of the Eucharist (*Apostolic Letter, Investigabiles divitias Christi*, February 5, 1965; cf. Appendix, HA 54).

96. Is there another statement of Pope Paul VI on the Sacred Heart and the Eucharist?

In the same Apostolic Letter the Holy Father wrote: "We especially desire, however, that through a more intense participation in the august Sacrament of the altar, a greater devotion be given to the Sacred Heart of Jesus, whose outstanding gift is the Eucharist" (Ibid., 53).

97. What did Pope Pius XII write on this point?

"It can therefore be declared that the divine Eucharist . . . and likewise the priesthood are indeed gifts of the Sacred Heart of Jesus. . . ." (HA 71) "Not the least part of the revelation of that Heart is the Eucharist, which he gave to us out of the great charity of his own Heart" (St. Albert the Great, quoted in HA no. 122).

98. What do you consider one of the best definitions of true devotion to the Sacred Heart of Jesus in relation to the Eucharist?

"The devotion to the Sacred Heart of Jesus is *a more warmhearted and ardent devotion towards Jesus Christ in the Blessed Sacrament*, its principal *motive* being the extreme love which he shows us in this Sacrament, and the principal *object*, to make reparation for the contempt which he undergoes in this same Sacrament. . . . a very ardent and tender love for the adorable Person of Jesus Christ ought to be the *fruit*."[1]

This is the definition given by Father Jean Croiset, S. J., who corresponded extensively with

---

[1] Jean Croiset, S. J., *Devotion to the Sacred Heart of Our Lord Jesus Christ* (Milwaukee: International Institute of the Heart of Jesus, 1976) 51. Cf. JRH, 195–266.

St. Margaret Mary, from whom he learned the true nature of this devotion as revealed to her by Our Lord himself.

99. Did the revelation at Paray-le-Monial have a eucharistic setting?

All the principal apparitions took place while St. Margaret Mary was praying before the Blessed Sacrament or after Communion.

100. Were Our Lord's requests eucharistic?

Yes. On one occasion he addressed to her these words, "I thirst . . . to be loved by men in the Blessed Sacrament. . . ." (JRH 133) He then indicated how we were to satisfy that thirst: 1) by the liturgical celebration of a feast in honor of and in reparation for the unrequited love of his Heart that moved him to institute the Eucharist; 2) by frequent Mass and Communion of reparation especially on the First Friday of each month "to make reparation for the insults he received during the month in the Blessed Sacrament" (Ibid.); 3) by eucharistic vigils of adoration and reparation.

101. Why does the practice of devotion to the Sacred Heart of Jesus lead to a greater devotion to the Person of Jesus Christ in the Eucharist?

1) This seems to be the special grace given to those who practice it. As Father Croiset stated (cf. Q 98): "A very ardent and tender love for the adorable Person of Jesus Christ ought to be the fruit;" for this devotion is "a more warm-hearted and ardent devotion towards Jesus Christ in the Blessed Sacrament."

2) It is a fact that indifference toward Christ in the Blessed Sacrament can be changed into love through the practice of devotion to the Heart of Jesus either personally or vicariously. One of the essential characteristics of this devotion is to convert indifferent and hardened hearts. Lukewarmness, coldness and sin are the principal reasons people stay away from Mass and Communion.

102. Would you say, then, that the practice of devotion to the Sacred Heart of Jesus is one of the best ways to build up eucharistic piety in individuals, in the family, in a parish?

Definitely, and a long experience proves how true this is.[2]

103. What are some of the eucharistic ways to practice this devotion as requested by Our Lord and encouraged by the Church?

[2] For some examples cf. ESH, Chap. 5, "The Argument of Facts".

1) *Yearly:* Celebration of the Solemnity of the Sacred Heart (Friday following Second Sunday after Pentecost).

2) *Monthly:* On the First Friday, Mass and Communion of reparation; Holy Hour in church or at home.

3) *Weekly:* Visits to the Blessed Sacrament, if it is not possible to go to Mass and Communion; Holy Hour.

4) *Daily:* Ideally, Mass and Communion or a visit to the Blessed Sacrament; Morning offering in union with the intentions of the eucharistic Heart of Jesus in the Mass; acts of charity towards the poor and lonely.

5) *Anytime:* Enthronement of the image of the Sacred Heart of Jesus as King and Friend in homes, in schools, in places of business, etc., and consecration to (covenant with) his loving Heart.

104. Can you give some quotations from spiritual writers about the Heart of Jesus and the Eucharist?

"Yes, I have found this Heart in the adorable Eucharist when I have found there the Heart of my King, of my Friend, of my Brother, that is to say, the Heart of my amiable Redeemer. And after that who will prevent me from praying with confidence and obtaining all that I shall ask?"[3]

"O most Sacred, most loving Heart of Jesus, Thou art concealed in the Holy Eucharist and Thou beatest for us still."[4]

"My devotion to the Blessed Sacrament and the Sacred Heart must permeate my whole life.... Everytime I hear anyone speak of the Sacred Heart of Jesus or of the Blessed Sacrament I feel an indescribable joy....

"I want the devotion to his Heart, concealed within the Sacrament of love to be the measure of all my spiritual progress.... My resolutions ... to do all ... in intimate union with the Sacred Heart of Jesus in the Blessed Sacrament.... These are loving appeals from Jesus who wants me wholeheartedly there, at the source of all goodness, his Sacred Heart, throbbing mysteriously behind the eucharistic veils."[5]

"The Eucharist is the sacrament of the Heart of Christ." (Karl Rahner, S. J.)

---

[3] St. Bernard, *Vita Mystica*, Cap. 111, Quoted by Rev. Jean Croiset, S. J., op. cit., 77.

[4] Henry Cardinal Newman, *Taking on the Heart of Christ* (New York: Dimension Books) 114.

[5] Pope John XXIII, *Journal of a Soul* (London: Geoffrey Chapman, 1965) 147–48.

"Find the Sacred Heart where it is, all good and all merciful, in the Eucharist . . . the Heart of Jesus that gave us Calvary and the Eucharist." (St. Peter Julian Eymard)[6]

105. Give an example of a prayer to the Heart of Jesus in the Eucharist.

"May the Heart of Jesus in the most Blessed Sacrament be praised, adored and loved, with grateful affection, at every moment, in all the tabernacles of the world, even to the end of time. Amen."

106. Is there a substantial difference between devotion to the Sacred Heart of Jesus and devotion to the eucharistic Heart?

No. The purpose of devotion to the eucharistic Heart of Jesus is simply to call our attention to the overflowing love of the Heart of our Savior which moved him to institute the Eucharist, the "Sacrament of love" (cf. HA no. 122). Likewise the expression "eucharistic Heart" reminds us that Jesus' Heart is truly present in the Blessed Sacrament.

---

[6] Quoted in Fr. Walter Kern, *Updated Devotion to the Sacred Heart* (Canfield, Ohio: Alba Books, 1974).

107. Did Pope Pius XII encourage us to practice devotion to the eucharistic Heart of Jesus?

Yes. "Nor will it be easy to understand the strength of the love which moved Christ to give himself to us as our spiritual food save by fostering in a special way the devotion to the eucharistic Heart of Jesus" (HA no. 122).

108. What did Cardinal Mario Luigi Ciappi, O. P. , Pro-theologian of the Pontifical House, say about this statement?

"With these words the Supreme Pontiff wished to spur all believers to the practice of the cult to the eucharistic Heart of Jesus, as it were to the choice of a surer and more direct way to penetrate the secrets of the mystery of the Eucharist."[7]

109. What other modern theologian has written in depth about devotion to the eucharistic Heart of Jesus?

Father Bertrand de Margerie, S. J. , S. T. D. , in *The Holy Spirit and the Daily Eucharist, Supreme Gifts of the Heart of Jesus*.[8]

---

[7] *The Eucharistic Heart of Jesus in the Light of the Encyclical* Haurietis Aquas *of Pope Pius XII* (Naples: Redemptorist Fathers, 1976).

[8] Milwaukee, Wisconsin: International Institute of the Heart of Jesus, 1976.

CHAPTER 10

THE HEART OF JESUS AND REPARATION

110. What is meant by "reparation"?

Reparation has several meanings: atonement, expiation, making amends, making up, penance, satisfaction, redress. In relation to God it means: "expiation offered by men to God for their own sins and the sins of others" (Webster).

111. In making reparation, what is repaired?

The damage done by man's sins to God's rights, to his honor and glory; to the bond of love between men and God, between man and his fellow man. As one little boy put it, "We repair the broken Heart of Jesus."

112. What role does reparation play in the practice of devotion to the Heart of Jesus?

Pope Pius XII taught us that devotion to the Sacred Heart of Jesus is "distinguished from other forms of Christian piety by the special qualities of love and reparation" (HA no. 95). Thus reparation may be said to be one of the essential characteristics of this devotion.

113. What did Pope Pius XI write about reparation?

In his encyclical "On Reparation Due to the Sacred Heart",[1] the Holy Father stated, "If in the act of consecration what stands out most is the intention to exchange, as it were, the love of us creatures for the love of the Creator, there follows almost naturally from this another fact, namely, that if this same uncreated love has either been passed over through forgetfulness or saddened by reason of our sins, then we should repair such offenses, no matter in what manner they have occurred. Ordinarily we call this duty reparation" (no. 8).

114. What obligations do we have to make reparation?

"We are held to the duty of making reparation by the most powerful motive of justice and love; of justice, in order to suffer together with Christ, patiently enduring insults and humiliations, so

[1] *Miserentissimus Redemptor* (*Acta Apostolica Sedis*, 20, 1928).

that we may bring to him, insofar as our human weakness permits, some comfort in his sufferings" (Ibid.).

115. In what sense can we speak of Christ's present "sufferings"?

In the sense understood by Pope Pius XI: "The sins committed now would be able of themselves to cause Christ to die a death accompanied by the same sufferings and agonies as his death on the Cross, since every sin must be said to renew in a certain sense the Passion of Our Lord, 'crucifying again to themselves the Son of God and making him a mockery' " (Ibid., no. 15).

116. How did Pope Pius XI explain "consoling" Christ?

"If, in view of our future sins, foreseen by him, the soul of Jesus became sad unto death, there can be no doubt that by his prevision at the same time of our acts of reparation, he was in some way comforted when 'there appeared to him an angel from Heaven' (Lk 22:43) to console that Heart of his bowed down with sorrow and anguish!" (Ibid., no. 15)

117. Did the Holy Father give another explanation?

Yes. "To the above we may add that the expiatory Passion of Jesus Christ is renewed and in a certain manner continued in his Mystical Body, the Church. . . . 'I am Jesus whom you are persecuting' (Acts 9:5). . . . Therefore, it is with reason that Christ, suffering in his Mystical Body, desires to have us as companions in his acts of expiation" (Ibid., no. 16).

118. In Our Lord's apparitions to St. Margaret Mary, did he request consolation?

Yes. In the third apparition of June, 1674. Here is the way St. Margaret Mary described what happened: "On one occasion, while the Blessed Sacrament was exposed, Jesus Christ presented himself to me all resplendent with glory, his five wounds shining like so many suns. Flames issued from every part of his sacred humanity, especially from his adorable breast, which resembled a furnace which, being opened, disclosed to me his most loving and lovable Heart, the living source of these flames. It was then he made known to me the marvels of his pure love and showed me to what excess he had loved men, from whom he received only ingratitude and contempt. 'I feel this more,' he said, 'than all that I suffered in my Passion. If only they would make some return for my love. . . . But they reject me and treat me with coldness. Do you at least console me by supplying for their ingratitude as far as you can.' "[2]

119. What form was this "consolation" or reparation to take, according to St. Margaret Mary?

First, by our return of love; in this way we "supply" for the ingratitude of others. Next, by certain eucharistic practices of reparation specified by Jesus himself: Masses and Communions of reparation, especially on the Feast of the Sacred Heart and on each First Friday; by the Holy Hour which can be made in church or at home (Ibid., 47).

120. What other forms of reparation are there?

Pope Pius XI enumerates the following: A person should "abhor and flee all sin as the greatest of all evils; offer oneself whole and entire to the Will of God; strive to repair the injured majesty of God by constant prayer, by voluntary penances, by patient suffering of all ills

[2] St. Margaret Mary, *Autobiography* (Baltimore: Newman Press, 1961) 46.

which shall befall him; in a word, he will organize his life that in all things it will be inspired by the spirit of reparation" (*Miserentissimus Redemptor*, no. 20).

121. *What about "social" reparation?*

By trying to rectify social injustices, we make reparation: likewise by acts of charity towards the poor, the underprivileged, discriminated minority groups.

CHAPTER 11

THE HEART OF JESUS—SOURCE AND SYMBOL OF UNITY

122. What did Pope Pius XII write about the Heart of Jesus in relation to unity in his Sacred Heart Encyclical, Haurietis Aquas?

"It is likewise Our most fervent desire that all who profess themselves Christians and are seriously engaged in the effort to establish the kingdom of Christ on earth will consider the practice of devotion to the Heart of Jesus as the source and symbol of unity, salvation and peace" (HA no. 122).

123. Why is the Heart of Jesus the "source and symbol of unity"?

It is the *source* of unity because it is the source of love, the principle and cause of unity. It is the *symbol* of unity because it is the symbol of that unbounded love which caused our Savior to shed his blood for all men, ". . . that they may be one, even as we are one" (Jn 17:11).

124. What connection is there between unity among Christians and the opening of Our Lord's Heart on Calvary?

St. Thomas Aquinas wrote: "From the side of Christ, there flowed water for cleansing, blood for redeeming. Hence blood is associated with the sacrament of the Eucharist, water with the sacrament of Baptism, which has its cleansing power by virtue of the blood of Christ" (cf. HA no. 76). These two sacraments are the means and signs of unity among Christians.

125. How does the practice of devotion to the Sacred Heart help effect unity?

Since the practice of this devotion increases love of God and neighbor, the answer is obvious. Moreover, the eucharistic piety which this devotion fosters in the hearts of those who practice it should lead to a greater unity with other men, for the Eucharist is both a sign and a cause of unity.

126. Did Our Lord promise unity at Paray-le-Monial?

Yes, in these words among many others: "Furthermore he promises by means of this devotion to his Divine Heart to reunite divided families, to protect those who are in any necessity, and to spread the sweet unction of his charity on all those religious communities where he is honored and which put themselves under his special protection. He will keep all hearts united so as to make them one with his own" (JRH 36, 131).

127. What did Pope St. Pius X say to the newly ordained Father Roncalli, the future Pope John, the Pope of unity?

"I will ask the good Lord to grant a special blessing on these good intentions of yours, so that you may really be a priest after his own Heart."[1]

128. What is the meaning of "a priest after Jesus' Heart"?

To be meek and humble: "Learn from me, for I am gentle and humble of heart" (Mt 11:29). These were the two virtues for which Pope John constantly prayed, strove, and which stood out in his life. This is the principal reason he was used as an instrument to unite all hearts with the Heart of Christ. It is significant that the Pope of

[1] *Journal of a Soul* (London: Geoffrey Chapman, 1965) 161.

the Sacred Heart was the one chosen by God to hold an ecumenical council. He was indeed the "Pope of unity".

129. What did Pope Paul VI write about the Sacred Heart and unity?

"It is moreover this Heart that moves the Church to look for all those means and helps which will return the separated brethren to full unity around the See of Peter. . . ." (Letter of May 25, 1965, to six Superior Generals)[2]

130. Is one of these means the Renewal of the Consecration of the human race to the Sacred Heart of Jesus first made by Pope Leo XIII in 1899?

Yes. In that Act of Consecration we read: "Be King of those deceived by erroneous opinions, or whom discord keeps aloof, and call them back to the harbor of truth and the unity of faith so that soon there may be but one flock and one shepherd." Pope Leo was moved to make this consecration by a letter he received from Mother [now Blessed] Mary of the Divine Heart, a German Good Shepherd nun, then stationed in Oportu, Portugal. She said Our Lord desired this

[2] *Diserti Interpretes Facti* (May 25, 1965). Cf. Appendix, HA 56.

consecration "in order to facilitate their [all baptized persons'] return to the true Church, as well as to hasten the spiritual birth of those unbaptized...." Pope Leo described this consecration as "the greatest act of my pontificate."[3] The Church prescribes the annual renewal of this consecration on the Feast of Christ the King in order to remind us that Jesus rules through his Heart, through love. The private and frequent renewal of this consecration is highly recommended, especially by those interested in ecumenism.

[3] Abbé Louis Chasle, *Sister Mary of the Divine Heart* (London: Burns & Oates, 1907).

Lucien —
- athlete
- character
- gentleman → team
- Soccer Cricket tennis
- bowling
- Nature — hiking — swimming
- gardening — music
- Xian home — Xmas friend Savior
- selfless — helping others
- putting others before self —

√ Ps. 121   Pr. of St. Francis

CHAPTER 12

THE HOLY SPIRIT: LIVING WATER FROM THE PIERCED HEART OF JESUS

131. How are the Heart of Jesus and the Holy Spirit interrelated?

The Holy Spirit, the third Person of the Holy Trinity, is the personal, mutual love of the Father and the Son. The Heart of Jesus is the symbol of the love of the second Person of the Blessed Trinity, the Son of God made man. Thus *love* is the link between "Heart" and "Spirit".

132. What role did the Holy Spirit play in the formation of the human heart of the God-Man?

As we read in the Litany of the Sacred Heart, the Heart of Jesus was "formed by the Holy Spirit in the womb of the Virgin Mary." This follows from the words of the Archangel Gabriel to Mary: "The Holy Spirit will come upon you..." (Lk 1:35) and of the Angel to Joseph: "...that which is conceived in her is of the Holy Spirit" (Mt 1:20).

133. Did the love of the Holy Spirit "overflow" into the human will and the Heart of Jesus?

Yes, together with the infinite love of the Father and the Son, as Pope Pius XII tells us, "The love of the Most Holy Trinity is the origin of man's redemption, it [love of the Father, Son, and the Holy Spirit] overflowed into the human will of Jesus Christ and into his adorable Heart with full efficacy...." (HA no. 89)

134. What did Pope Pius XII write about the Holy Spirit as a gift of the Heart of Jesus?

"The gift of the Holy Spirit, sent upon his disciples, is the first notable sign of his abounding charity after his triumphant ascent to the right hand of his Father" (HA no. 81).

135. What did a Franciscan, Father Stephan Fridolin, write about the Holy Spirit as a gift of the Heart of Jesus, some 500 years ago?

"To say nothing of the other blessings which we owe to the Sacred Heart, it has given us one gift in which all others are included; this is the Holy Spirit, the substantial gift of God" (HS 96).

136. What did this same Franciscan write about the manner in which the Holy Spirit dwells in the Heart of Jesus?

"The Heart of Christ is the worthiest and purest of all the dwellings of the Holy Spirit, for he does not dwell there simply through the workings of grace, nor for a limited length of time, as with other men, but essentially, unceasingly, in the perfect exercise of all his operations and all his virtues, without the slightest imperfection. He dwells there always and for all eternity" (HS 96).

137. When did Jesus speak of his Heart as the source of "living water"?

On the Feast of Tabernacles, when Jesus promised "living water" (Jn 7:37–39).

138. What did Jesus mean by the expression "living water"?

"Living water" means the Holy Spirit, as St. John tells us: "If anyone thirsts let him come to me, let him who believes in me drink. As the

Scripture has said: 'Out of his heart shall flow rivers of living water.' Now this he said about the Spirit, which those who believe in him were to receive for as yet the Spirit had not been given, because Jesus was not yet glorified" (Jn 7:37–39).

139. When was this promise fulfilled?

When Jesus' Heart was opened after his death: "But one of the soldiers pierced his side with a lance and immediately there came out blood and water" (Jn 19:34).

140. Was this outpouring of blood and water a fulfillment of an Old Testament prophecy, recalled on the last day of the Feast of Tabernacles?

Yes, that of Zechariah (13:1): "On that day there shall be a fountain opened for the House of David and the inhabitants of Jerusalem to cleanse them from sin and uncleanness." As Father Hugo Rahner writes: "Connect this text with that which immediately precedes it (the revelation of the Messiah as the 'pierced one' and of the 'pouring out of the spirit of grace on the inhabitants of Jerusalem' (Zech 12:10), and you find yourself in those paths of scriptural understanding at which Our Lord himself was hinting when he cried: 'The Scripture says: Streams of living water shall spring from the Heart of the Messiah'" (HS 32).

141. In reference to the above statement of St. John that "Jesus was not yet glorified", when did this "glorification" take place?

Again quoting Father Rahner: " 'Glorification' here connotes the Messianic Passion and death (Jn 12:28; 13:31; 17:4) together with the bodily transformation which can be attained only in this way. The gift of the Redeemer is therefore the Spirit which he has released to us through the sacrifice of his life. . . . All the predictions of this seventh chapter of St. John are fulfilled in the instant that Christ's Heart is pierced on the Cross (Jn 19:34)" (HS 32).

142. What did Pope Pius XII write about the Old Testament prophecies concerning the promise of Jesus to bestow "living water on those who believe in him"?

"For those who are listening to Jesus speaking, it certainly was not difficult to relate these words by which he promised a fountain of 'living water' destined to spring from his own side to the words of sacred prophecy of Isaiah, Ezekiel, and

Zechariah, foretelling the Messianic Kingdom and likewise to the symbolic rock from which, when struck by Moses, water flowed forth in a miraculous manner" (HA no. 4).

143. What are these three prophecies to which Pope Pius refers?

1) "With joy you will draw water from the wells of salvation" (Is 12:3). (This is the title of the Sacred Heart Encyclical—in Latin: *Haurietis Aquas*—"You will draw waters. . .").

2) ". . .and behold, water was issuing from below the threshold of the temple. . . ." (Ezek 47:1–2)

3) "On that day shall be a fountain opened." (Zech 13:1)

144. What is the meaning of the reference to the "symbolic rock" struck by Moses?

"As Moses, the first savior, caused the spring to flow [from a rock], so too the second Savior, the Messiah, will open a 'fountain of water'. Jesus, by his death, brought to fulfillment the Jews' hope for salvation, for his Heart is that cloven rock from which spring the living waters of the Spirit. As St. Paul tells us (1 Cor 10:4), 'The rock was Christ' " (HS 32).

145. What did Justin Martyr write about "living water" and the Heart of Jesus less than 200 years after the death of Christ?

"We Christians are the true Israel which springs from Christ; we are carved out of his Heart (*koilia*) as from a rock. . . . He makes living water overflow into the hearts of those who through him love the Father of the universe, and he satiates those who drink the water of life" (From *Dialogue* 135, 5. Quoted by Father H. Rahner in HS 45).

146. Are there other testimonies concerning "living water" and the Heart of Jesus from the same period?

In a letter from Lyons concerning the martyrdom of the Deacon Sanctus, a member of the Church of Lyons sent this letter to his brethren in the faith in Asia Minor: "But he remained unshaken and steadfast, unyielding he persevered in his confession. For like a gentle and strengthening dew from heaven there flowed onto him that living water which goes forth from the Heart of Christ" (HS 44).

147. What did Origen write about St. John "drinking" of the living water?

He makes the Apostle John "drink at the

Heart of Our Lord the streams of living water" (*Commentary on the Canticles* I, cf. HS 50).

148. Did any other writer of that period state more or less the same idea?

In the fifth century, Paulinus of Nola wrote in his *Tract on St. John* (18, 1): "John, who rested blissfully on the breast of Our Lord, was inebriated with the Holy Spirit: from the heart of the all-creating Wisdom he quaffed an understanding which transcends that of any creature" (HS 51).

149. An "understanding" of what?

Of the meaning of St. John's own sublime statements: *God is Love* (1 Jn 4:7): "We love because he first loved us" (1 Jn 4:19). John is the apostle of love. He was filled with the Holy Spirit, the spirit of love, which he received when he rested his head on Jesus' breast and heard the beatings of his Sacred Heart.

150. How can I increase my understanding of and love for the Heart of Jesus?

1) Each time you participate in the Holy Sacrifice of the Mass, Jesus, from his ever-open Heart, pours into your heart—provided it is open and receptive—his Holy Spirit, the spirit

of understanding, of wisdom, knowledge, and especially of love.

2) When you receive Jesus in Communion, like St. John, you can "rest your head" on his Heart. Better still, you can unite your heart with his, asking the Holy Spirit to "enkindle in me the fire of divine love."

3) Praying daily to the Holy Spirit (especially the prayer beginning "Come Holy Spirit, fill the hearts of your faithful. . . .") that he may help you to understand and to love the Heart of Jesus and to draw from it the inspiration and courage you need.

151. Please explain the interrelationship of the Holy Spirit and the Immaculate Heart of Mary.

When the Angel Gabriel appeared to Mary to announce that she was to become the mother of the Messiah, he said, "The Holy Spirit will come upon you. . . ." (Lk 1:35) The opening prayer for the Mass of the Immaculate Heart of Mary explains further: "Father, you prepared the heart of the Virgin Mary to be a fitting home for your Holy Spirit. . . ."[1]

---

[1] Cf. Pope Paul VI, *Marialis Cultus* (Boston: St. Paul Publications, 1974) 24 ff.

152. Was St. Margaret Mary an "instrument" of the Holy Spirit?

Yes. As Father Stierli writes in *Heart of the Savior* (209), "It is the same Holy Spirit who, through St. Margaret Mary, and through the mouth of the Church, directs us so insistently to the mystery of the Heart of Jesus."

153. Was Father Mateo, the "Apostle of the Sacred Heart", also an apostle of the Holy Spirit?

Very much so. It was he who initiated and encouraged for many long years the "Rosary of the Holy Spirit" (cf. ESH 517). One of his favorite prayers was, "Come Holy Spirit, enlighten my mind, inflame my heart!" Another (a part of the Rosary of the Holy Spirit), "Father, Father, send us the promised Paraclete, through Jesus Christ Our Lord. Amen."

154. What is the conclusion of all this?

If we follow the living waters to their source, we will come to the pierced Heart of the Savior; for it is the opened Heart of Jesus that gives us the Holy Spirit. As Father Hugo Rahner writes (HS 34): "Since the day of Pentecost, the graces won for us by the Heart of Jesus, broken in death, have been flowing to us with the living water from the wounded side of our glorified Lord."

CHAPTER 13

VATICAN II AND THE HEART OF JESUS

155. What did the Council documents say about the Sacred Heart?

"The Son of God ... loved us with a human heart" (*The Church Today*, Chap. 1, no. 22).

156. Did Pope Paul VI, official interpreter of the Council documents, issue any statement after Vatican II, explaining the importance of devotion to the Sacred Heart in carrying out the directives of the Vatican Council?

In 1965, the Holy Father issued two letters on this subject: *Investigabiles Divitias Christi (IDC)*, a pastoral letter to the bishops of the world, dated February 6, 1965, and *Diserti Interpretes Facti (DIF)*, May 25, 1965, a development of the ideas contained in the first Letter.

157. What are some of the pertinent texts of these two documents?

1) *Timeliness*: "This therefore seems to us to be the most suitable ideal: that devotion to the Sacred Heart . . . now reflourish daily more and more. Let it be esteemed by all as an acceptable form of true piety, which in our times, especially because of the norms laid down by the Second Vatican Council, must be rendered to Christ Jesus, 'the King and Center of all hearts. . . .' " (Col 1:18) (IDC)

2) *Importance*: "It is absolutely necessary that the faithful venerate and honor this Heart, in the expression of their private piety as well as in the services of public cult. . . . (DIF)

3) *Eucharist*: "We especially desire, however, that through a more intense participation in the august Sacrament of the altar, a greater devotion be given to the Sacred Heart of Jesus, whose outstanding gift is the Eucharist" (DIF).

4) *Liturgy*: "The origin and principle of the Sacred Liturgy is found there [in the Sacred Heart], for the Heart of Jesus is the sacred temple of God from which there ascends to the eternal Father the expiatory sacrifice. . . ."(DIF)

5). *Missionary zeal*: "She [the Church] finds there [in the Sacred Heart] the drive to bring it about that those who as yet cannot claim the name of Christian, may know with us 'the only true God and him whom he sent, Jesus Christ' " (Jn 17:3) (DIF).

6) *Mystery of the Church*: "For, as everyone knows, the Sacred Council aims especially at bringing about this restoration of discipline, public as well as private, in every corner and field of the Christian life. For this reason it has brought to light the brilliant mystery of the Holy Church. But this mystery can never be properly understood if the attention of the people is not drawn to the eternal love of the Incarnate Word, of which the wounded Heart of Jesus is the outstanding symbol: for, as we read in the dogmatic constitution which bears its name, 'The Church, or, in other words, the kingdom of Christ now present in mystery, grows visibly through the power of God in the world. This inauguration and this growth are both symbolized by the blood and water which flowed from the open side of a crucified Jesus' (*On the Church*, no. 3). For the Church was born from the pierced Heart of the Redeemer, and is nourished there, for 'Christ loved the Church and delivered himself up for her, that he might sanctify her in the bath of water by means of the word' (Eph 5:25–26)" (DIF).

158. Where can I find these letters?

They are contained in the appendix to the Sa-

Jesus the perfect fulfillment of my every desire, of my greatest expectation

Jesus is incompatible

cred Heart Encyclical of Pius XII, *Haurietis Aquas*.[1]

159. What else did Pope Paul VI say about the symbolism of the Sacred Heart for moderns?

On January 27, 1971, in the general audience, he spoke these words: "Mystical understanding came to contemplate him in the heart; it has made devotion to the Sacred Heart the fiery furnace and symbol of Christian devotion and activity for us moderns, who value feelings and psychology, and are always oriented towards the metaphysics of love."

[1] International Institute of the Heart of Jesus, Milwaukee Wisconsin 53213.

CHAPTER 14

THE HEART OF JESUS AND THE "DOMESTIC CHURCH"

160. What constitutes the heart of the home?

Love: a home without love is like a body without a heart.

161. What brings love into a home?

A team: God and the parents. Love keeps God in the home, but the presence of Christ in the home also keeps love in the family. Where there is love, there is God. Without his presence and help, however, the family is helpless to keep love for God in their family life: "Without me you can do nothing" (Jn 15:5).

162. Do families need special help to keep the love of God in their homes or to regain it if it has grown cold or has been lost?

Given the many forces at work today to undermine and destroy the Christian family, it is obvious that extraordinary supernatural help is needed to preserve and strengthen family life.

163. What spiritual means do you recommend to families to help solve their problems?

1) Married couples should remember that when they received the Sacrament of Matrimony they entered into a bilateral contract not only with each other, but with Almighty God. This means that they are assured of the necessary graces needed to cope with each family crisis and problem. Consequently, married couples should trustingly call upon God, their loving Father, to grant them the helps they need.

2) They should bring the presence of Christ into their home by family prayer (especially the Rosary) or by Scripture reading in common, for Jesus promised that he would be present wherever two or more are gathered together in his name.

3) They should share in the powerful graces to be found in frequent Mass and Communion.

164. Any other suggestions?

The Enthronement of the Sacred Heart (that is, of Jesus) is an effective way to create the right atmosphere for prayer in the home; to actualize the potential the family has for a stronger Christian family life; to bring the family closer to the Person of Christ in the Eucharist; to help make the family a "little Church", a "domestic Church", that is, a praying family, a worshipping family, a "community of love".

165. Briefly, what is the Enthronement of the Sacred Heart in the home?

The word "enthronement" means "to place on a throne in recognition of someone's authority." In this case it is the authority of God which is proclaimed. The expression "Sacred Heart" refers to the Person of Christ, whose divine-human love is symbolized by his human and "sacred" Heart. The "Enthronement of the Sacred Heart", then, is a ceremony in which the head of the house enthrones an image of the Sacred Heart of Jesus in a conspicuous place in the home as a public recognition of the authority of Christ the Lord, the King of Love. It is followed by the Creed and an act of family consecration, which is like a pact or covenant of love between the family and the Heart of Jesus.

166. Is this all there is to the Enthronement?

No, the ceremony is the beginning of a new way of life, of a strong Christian family life. It helps to bring about a greater union of hearts in the family, a greater love between the Heart of Jesus and the hearts of the parents and children, a more intimate sharing with Jesus, the Lord and Friend of the family.

167. What brings this about?

The fidelity of the Sacred Heart of Jesus to his promises and the good will and cooperation of at least some members of the family.

168. What are some of the promises of Jesus?

All stem from the Gospel: "Seek first the kingdom of God and his justice and all other things will be given you besides" (Mt 6:33). "For where two or three meet in my name, I shall be there with them" (Mt 18:20). At Paray-le-Monial Our Lord was more specific and attached special graces to the honoring of his Heart through trustful love, fidelity to duty, the Eucharist, and by carrying out his requests.

169. What are some of these requests?

1) Participation in the Holy Sacrifice of the Mass through Communion received in a spirit of eucharistic reparation.

2) A deeper, personal, more grateful love for him, especially in the Blessed Sacrament.

3) Consecrating ourselves to his Sacred Heart.

4) Exposing and honoring the image of Jesus' human, glorified Heart as an act of loving gratitude and reparation.

170. What did Jesus promise families in return?

He promised: "He will unite divided families. . . . He will bless all their undertakings. . . . He will give them security in life and at the hour of death. . . . He will bring peace to their families. . . . He will change tepidity and unconcern to greater generosity. . . . He will soften the hardest hearts" (JRH 35, 31, 131, 141).

171. Why did Jesus make these promises?

Because his Heart is overflowing with merciful love for us poor sinners: "My Heart is moved with pity for the crowd" (Mk 8:2).

172. What disposition must a family have for the fulfillment of these promises?

Good will, trust in God's love and his fidelity to his promises, and a serious sustained effort to be generous in carrying out the commandments of God and his Church, and one's daily duties according to each one's state in life.

173. Is there a book available that explains the Enthronement and gives examples of actual cases of families whose lives have been changed or bettered through the Enthronement of the Sacred Heart in their homes?

The *Enthronement of the Sacred Heart* (ESH) is such a book. In its pages also will be found chapters on the doctrine of and devotion to the Heart of Jesus, explained in a popular way; on the promises of the Sacred Heart; on Night Adoration in the home, with many true stories of conversions and other graces received; Tarcisians of the Sacred Heart; prayers and devotions in honor of the Sacred Heart of Jesus and the Immaculate Heart of Mary; the Sacred Heart Encyclical of Pope Pius XII, and much more.

174. What rituals for the Enthronement of the Sacred Heart in the home are available?

There is the traditional ritual, which may be carried out with or without a priest. It is contained in a short pamphlet with preliminary explanations, called *Thy Kingdom Come* (TKC). There is the *Family Enthronement Covenant* (DIY), written especially for the ceremony when a priest is not present.

175. May the Enthronement be combined with Mass in the home?

Yes. There is available a special missalette containing the Mass of the Sacred Heart. The Enthronement ceremony may either precede the Mass or come after the homily. The Act of Consecration is called "Family Covenant with God", thereby linking the family covenant with renewal of Jesus' covenant in the Sacrifice of the Mass.

176. What other Enthronement rituals are available?

There are rituals for rectories, convents, schools, places of business, institutions. Most of the above will be found in the book *Enthronement of the Sacred Heart*. They are also available separately.

A new ritual has recently been published. It is called "Celebration of the Enthronement of Jesus as Lord of the Home." It is appropriate for charismatic-oriented families and others looking for a contemporary Enthronement ceremonial.[1]

[1] All the above-mentioned rituals may be obtained from The National Enthronement Center, Fairhaven, Mass. 02719. A catalogue will be sent on request.

CHAPTER 15

SACRED HEART APOSTOLATES

177. Is there a Sacred Heart apostolate for youth?

Yes. It is called "Tarcisians of the Sacred Heart", also known as "Tarcisian Clubs".

178. What is its aim?

To spread the reign of the Sacred Heart of Jesus, through the Enthronement-Covenant in the home.

179. What means do Tarcisians use to accomplish this goal?

They earn spiritual "Golden Pennies" consisting of prayers, sacrifices, eucharistic practices, all performed out of love (thereby changing them into spiritual "gold") and which they offer to the Heart of Jesus in "payment" for the conversion of sinners, and for the reign of the Sacred Heart in the home and in the missions.

180. Where may one obtain more details about this children's apostolate?

In the book, *Enthronement of the Sacred Heart*, and in the literature available at the National Center, or at authorized centers.

181. Are there other apostolates which help promote the reign of the Sacred Heart of Jesus?

Several. One of them is Night Adoration in the Home, which calls for a Holy Hour in the home (or any other living quarters) once a month between 9:00 P.M. and 6:00 A.M. Another is the Apostolate of Suffering. Members offer their moral, physical, or mental sufferings to the Heart of Jesus that his reign of merciful love may be established in hearts and homes.

182. Is there a special association for laymen?

Yes. It is called "The Men of the Sacred Heart" (MSH). Members are men who have had the Sacred Heart enthroned in their homes and who want to share with other families the graces they and their families have received. The Enthronement of the Sacred Heart in homes is their principal apostolate, but they also work and pray for the Enthronement in schools, in other institutions, and in places of business. Both married and single men belong. The MSH are likewise involved in other apostolic works such as pro-life movements, etc.[1]

183. Structurally, how are they organized; where are they located?

The MSH have a National Office, a National Council, and Local and Regional Chapters, which have their own officers.

184. Where there is no MSH Chapter, may a man become a member?

Yes. Any man working on his own promoting the Enthronement or devotion to the Sacred Heart is invited to join. By so doing, he associates himself spiritually with other men and so shares in their prayers and sacrifices. Members of the MSH keep in touch with one another by means of a newsletter.

185. To whom should I write for further information about the MSH?

To The National Secretary General, P.O. Box 4367, Santa Clara, CA 95054.

---

[1] For further information, write to Rev. Francis Larkin, SS. CC., Fairhaven, Mass. 02719.

186. What is the Apostleship of Prayer?

The *Apostleship of Prayer* "is people united in love with Christ and praying for the causes which Christ has at heart today. They pray mainly by offering themselves in the Mass, by renewing this offering in their daily offering prayer, and by living out this offering in all the thoughts, words, activities, and sufferings of their day" (cf. Father Walter Kern, *Updated Devotion to the Sacred Heart* [1974]).

CHAPTER 16

THE HEART OF JESUS AND THE IMMACULATE HEART OF MARY

187. What did Pope Pius XII write in Haurietis Aquas *about the devotion to the Immaculate Heart of Mary and its relation to the devotion to the Sacred Heart of Jesus?*

"In order that favors may flow in greater abundance on all Christians, even on the whole human race, from the devotion to the Most Sacred Heart of Jesus, let the faithful see to it that devotion to the Immaculate Heart of the Mother of God be closely joined to devotion to the Sacred Heart of Jesus" (HA no. 124).

188. What reason did the Holy Father give to justify this statement?

"By God's will, in carrying out the work of human redemption the Blessed Virgin Mary was inseparably linked with Christ in such a manner that our salvation sprang from the love and the sufferings of Jesus Christ to which the love and sorrows of his Mother were intimately united" (HA no. 124).

189. What else did Pope Pius XII say on this subject?

"It is, then, entirely fitting that the Christian people—who received the divine life from Christ through Mary—after they have paid their debt of honor to the Sacred Heart of Jesus, should also offer to the most loving Heart of their heavenly Mother the corresponding acts of piety, affection, gratitude and expiation" (HA no. 124).

190. Did the same Pope consecrate the Church and the whole world to the Immaculate Heart of Mary?

Yes, in 1942. Of this act, he wrote in the Sacred Heart Encyclical: "Entirely in keeping with this most kind and wise disposition of Divine Providence is the memorable act of consecration by which We ourselves solemnly dedicated Holy Church and the whole world to the spotless Heart of the Blessed Virgin Mary" (HA no. 124).

191. What other relationships are there between these two devotions?

In his manual, *Religious of the Sacred Hearts*, Father Marie-Bernard Garrie, SS. CC., wrote: "The Heart of Jesus is the goal, the Heart of Mary is the way; the Heart of Jesus is the sanctuary, the Heart of Mary is the gate." He then quotes Father Marie Joseph Coudrin, SS. CC., founder of the Congregation of the Sacred Hearts, who said: "The Heart of Mary has been pierced so that through it, all might pass; the Heart of Jesus has been opened so that in it, all might abide."

192. What did Our Lady say about her Immaculate Heart at Fatima?

She said to make sacrifices for sinners and to say many times: "O Jesus, it is for your love, for the conversion of sinners, and in reparation for the sins committed against my Immaculate Heart." On another occasion, when speaking of saving sinners from hell, she said that "God wishes to establish in the world devotion to my Immaculate Heart." And, after predicting various punishments resulting from sin, she promised: "In the end, my Immaculate Heart will triumph."

193. Is there anything else?

Yes, the most important of all: Our Lady begged us at Fatima to "stop offending my Son Jesus"; to fulfill the duties of our state in life in a spirit of reparation; to pray the Rosary and meditate on the mysteries of the life of Jesus, and offer prayers and sacrifices for the conversion of sinners (OLF).

Our Lady further requested that we receive Communion on five First Saturdays of the month in a spirit of reparation.

194. Why five First Saturday Communions of reparation?

Here is Our Lord's own reply, reportedly given to Sister Lucia of Fatima, on May 29-30, 1930: "There are five kinds of offenses committed against the Immaculate Heart of Mary:

1) Against her Immaculate Conception;

2) Against her virginity:

3) Against her Divine Maternity, at the same time refusing to accept her as the Mother of mankind;

4) Those who try to put into hearts of children

forms of rejection of Mary, indifference and even hatred for this Immaculate Mother;

5) Those who offend her personally by their treatment of her sacred images."

195. What is the significance of this reply today?

This remarkable statement, made known by Lucia's confessor and published in *Broteria*, a Lisbon Jesuit magazine, and in *L'Appel de Notre Dame*, Paris, in 1968, is both an accurate prophecy of what is sadly happening today and—more importantly—what Jesus wants us to do about it.

The next time you learn of any person, group, or writing, offending Mary's Heart in any one of these five ways, carry out—and persuade others to do the same—Our Lord's request and receive him in Communion on First Saturdays. This is the way to act towards those who offend Our Lady. How much better than criticizing, condemning, or doing nothing!

(Note: Our Lord also made it known to Lucia that for just reasons a priest may transfer this Communion to a Sunday.)

196. What did Jesus promise in return?

Jesus promised that as a result of this eucharistic act of reparation in honor of the Immaculate Heart of his Mother, he would be moved to grant forgiveness to those persons who have the misfortune to offend her.

197. What was the promise made to Lucia by Our Lady in 1925?

"I promise to assist at the hour of death, with the graces necessary for salvation, all those who on the First Saturday of five consecutive months go to confession and receive Holy Communion."

198. Can you suggest a prayer to the Immaculate Heart of Mary?

Here is one of many: "O God of goodness, who filled the pure and holy Heart of Mary with the same sentiments of mercy and tenderness that filled the Heart of Jesus, grant, we beseech you, to all who honor her Immaculate Heart, the grace to keep until death a perfect conformity with the Sacred Heart of Jesus Christ, who lives and reigns with you and the Holy Spirit, world without end. Amen."

199. What aspirations do you recommend?

"Immaculate Heart of Mary, most sweet and compassionate, be our consolation in the sorrows of this life, and our refuge at the hour of death."

"Immaculate and Sorrowful Heart of Mary, pray for us now and at the hour of our death. Amen."

"Sweet Heart of Mary, be my salvation."

200. Where can I find other prayers, acts of consecration to the Immaculate Heart of Mary; also the formula of consecration of families to the Immaculate Heart of Mary?

In the book *Enthronement of the Sacred Heart*, 525 ff.

201. Did St. Margaret Mary speak about the Immaculate Heart of Mary?

Yes, many times. For instance, she recommended to her novices to offer to the Eternal Father, on the altar of Mary's Heart, the sacrifices which his divine Son continues to present to him. She composed a prayer that begins, "O Sacred Hearts of Jesus and Mary, repair all our shortcomings . . . enkindle in our hearts your flame of love."

202. What about Blessed Claude la Colombière, S. J., her spiritual director—did he too honor the Immaculate Heart of Mary?

Yes. Here is one of many examples: "I wish that my heart be always in the Hearts of Jesus and Mary."

203. Can you give examples of the devotion to the Immaculate Heart of Mary on the part of other great lovers of the Sacred Heart?

There are many, for instance:

St. Gertrude, O. S. B. (13th c.), "Theologian of the Sacred Heart", asked forgiveness for her sins through the abundant tenderness of the Heart of Mary.

St. Mechtilde (14th c.) received from Our Lord the command to honor the Heart of Mary as "the most humble, the most loving, and the most peaceful of hearts."

St. John Eudes (17th c.) was proclaimed by Pope St. Pius X as "The Doctor and Apostle of the liturgical cult of the Hearts of Jesus and Mary."

Fr. Mateo Crawley-Boevey, SS. CC., from the very beginning of his crusade of the Enthronement of the Sacred Heart, included the mediation of the Immaculate Heart of Mary in the ceremony of the Enthronement he composed for families in 1907.

204. What is your conclusion?

In the words attributed to Our Lady at Fatima, Jesus does not want devotion to his Heart separated from devotion to the Immaculate Heart of his Mother.

205. What is the full title of the Congregation whose initials are SS. CC. ?

"SS. CC." are the initials of the Latin words SACRORUM CORDIUM—"of the Sacred Hearts". The full title is "Congregation of the Sacred Hearts of Jesus and Mary and of Perpetual Adoration". It was founded in 1800 in France. (A sketch of this Congregation is found in the book *Enthronement of the Sacred Heart*, 227 ff.).

206. Are there any books by Fr. Mateo Crawley-Boevey, SS. CC. [Founder of the Enthronement, Night Adoration in the Home, and the Tarcisians of the Sacred Heart] which are available?

Yes: *Jesus King of Love*, down-to-earth conferences on the merciful love of the Sacred Heart of Jesus manifested in the Gospels, in the Eucharist—a spiritual classic.

Twenty Holy Hours, unique dialogues with

Jesus in the Eucharist, suitable for use in the home, church or chapel.[1]

The stirring story of his unusual apostolic career has been published under the title, *The Firebrand*, with fifty photographs.[2]

207. Can you recommend a recent book on devotion to the Sacred Heart?

Yes. *Updated Devotion to the Sacred Heart*, by Father Walter Kern.[3] It contains a complete, though brief, history of the devotion; its scriptural, theological and liturgical basis; the teaching of the magisterium, and the insights of modern theology; and a collection of traditional and contemporary prayers. An Enthronement ritual is also included. Highly recommended.

208. What is your final conclusion about the importance of the practice of devotion to the Sacred Heart in the world of today?

I make my own the challenging reflections of Father Josef Stierli, S. J. :

> The Heart of Jesus is a Heart of purest love, for love forms the very center of his Person and the

[1] These two books have been reprinted in English and Spanish by the Daughters of St. Paul. They also publish *The Trailblazer*, Father Mateo's life story for youth.
[2] National Enthronment Center, Fairhaven, Mass. 02719.
[3] Canfield, Ohio: Alba Books, 1975.

driving force of his life and death. Love is, therefore, the soul of Christianity and of the Christian life. In the very center of our faith stands the mighty phrase of St. John that God is Love; and we experience for ourselves the blessed truth that he is also wholly love for us. So we must try to realize, not just intellectually, but from the depths of our hearts, that we should love him and that we may love him "with our whole heart".

But both the love of God for men and the love of men for God are movingly revealed in the pierced Heart of Christ on the Cross: the wonderful love of the Father and the dedicated love of the Son.

No doubt other mysteries are capable of kindling men's love for God, because they too are revelations of love: the crib of Bethlehem, the Way of the Cross to Golgotha, the miracle of the Blessed Eucharist. But in the Heart of our Lord we meet in its most arresting form the sum and substance of all the revelations of God's, Love. That is why this sign and this mystery of the Heart has been given with a special urgency to our age, when "love has grown cold". It should challenge us to a warm love for God and men, which will fill our hearts and inspire all our actions. This mystery of the Sacred Heart not only throws down the challenge, but it imparts enthusiasm and strength to those who take it up. Our Christianity has grown too sober. We would be better for some of the holy intoxication of that Spirit of Pentecost whom we find in the Heart of Jesus.

All honor to the Code of Canon Law and the organization of the Church; they fulfill an essential function in the Kingdom of God. But they are never going to set the world on fire. Only love can do that—or hatred. And because hatred toils with such diabolical energy, love is called forth for a last encounter. The wellsprings of our human love have run dry; but their divine source flows untiringly from the pierced Heart of Christ on the cross.

One last benefit of the devotion remains to be indicated, one that includes all the others and gives them their full meaning: a deep personal union of a human heart with the Heart of Christ. . . . It is in this devotion that Christianity is revealed as a truly personal religion; for at its center stands a person, who is envisaged not only in his outward aspects, but in his Heart, the center and source of his personality.[4]

[4] *Heart of the Savior*, 207–208.

APPENDIX

FAMILY ENTHRONEMENT RITUAL

JESUS CHRIST IS LORD!

Celebration of the Enthronement of Jesus As Lord of the Family[1]

I

The Enthronement Ritual is a paraliturgical family celebration in which Jesus Christ is proclaimed the Lord of the home. In this celebration there are two essential elements:

1. The *installation* of a representation of the glorified Heart of Jesus the *Lord* in a prominent place in the home. Preferably this is done by the father who thus exercises his priestly role as religious leader in the family. From this act the word "Enthronement" takes its name.

2. The *consecration* of the family to the Heart of Jesus its *Friend*. This consecration by which the

---

[1] Non-Catholics may adapt the wording of this ritual as needed.

family is "set aside" as something holy and pleasing to the Lord, is also a voluntary *dedication*, a "turning over" of the family to Jesus, its rightful Head. The consecration is, moreover, a *covenant*, a pact, which the family freely makes with the Heart of Jesus: "All that the Lord has spoken we will do, and we will be obedient" (Ex 24:7). This covenant is like a collective renewal of the baptismal commitment made by each member of the family.

II

The Enthronement both as a celebration and as a program of daily family spirituality has certain basic characteristics.

Scriptural

The Enthronement concept is rooted in Scripture. The theme of the enthroned Lord ruling his people runs all through the Old Testament: *"But the Lord sits enthroned forever. . . . Sing praise to the Lord enthroned in Zion"* (Ps 9). *"God is enthroned as King forever"* (Ps 28). In the New Testament Jesus frequently speaks about his Kingdom: *"But seek first his kingdom and his righteousness. . . ."* (Mt 6:33) Before Pilate he openly professed his kingship: *"You say that I am a King"* (Jn 18:37).

Jesus' love for the family stands out in the Gospels: Nazareth, Cana, Bethany are familiar symbols of this love. To Zaccheus the sinner Jesus said, *"I must stay in your house today"* (Lk 29:5). In Revelation we read: *"Behold, I stand at the door and knock; if anyone hears my voice and opens the door, I will come in to him and eat with him and he with me"* (Rev 3:20). The ideal of the Enthronement program is to make the homes of today other Nazareths, Canas, Bethanies, wherein Jesus is acknowledged as Lord and is loved as a Friend. To familiarize families with these truths, daily Bible reading is strongly encouraged: *"Learn to know the Heart of God in the Word of God"* (St. Gregory the Great).

Paraliturgical/Liturgical

Vatican II, and more recently, Popes Paul VI, John Paul I, and John Paul II, have described the family as a "domestic church", a phrase first used by Saints Augustine and John Chrysostom. Pope John Paul I, in his only talk to American bishops,[2] stated: "Through family prayer the *ecclesia domestica* (domestic church) becomes an effective reality and leads to the transformation of the world." The Enthronement program calls for daily family prayer, especially the family

[2] Cf. *L'Osservatore Romano* (Sept. 28, 1978).

Rosary, and daily renewal of the family covenant at the evening meal. Likewise, both as an introductory ceremony and an on-going family life style, the Enthronement is a form of family worship in the domestic church. This truth is enhanced when the Enthronement takes place in conjunction with Mass in the home. (There is a special missalette for this purpose.)[3] The Enthronement brings into the family the spirit of the great liturgical celebrations of *Christ the King* (loyalty/obedience), *Sacred Heart* (love, Eucharist/reparation), *Holy Family* (charity/peace/unity).

The practice of true devotion to the Heart of Jesus necessarily results in a more active participation in the eucharistic liturgy. If we consider this devotion's principal practices, the reason is obvious: annual celebration of the liturgy of the Sacred Heart, First Friday Mass and Communion, exposition and eucharistic vigils. Finally, experience proves that those who sincerely and consistently practice this devotion to the Heart of Jesus receive the special graces of conversion from sin and increase of faith in and love for the Blessed Sacrament. "Before men can come to the liturgy," Vatican II reminds us, "they must be

[3] National Enthronement Center, Fairhaven, Mass. 02719. Ask for EN-MASS-2.

called to faith and to conversion." This, precisely, is what devotion to the Sacred Heart in the home brings about, especially when it becomes an integral part of everyday family spirituality.

Prayerful

The practice of devotion to the Sacred Heart of Jesus in the family circle increases love for Jesus and thereby encourages family prayer, which can be called an "exchange of love". Praying together keeps Christ present in the home: *"For where two or three are gathered in my name, there I am in the midst of them"* (Mt 18:20). Thus present in the very center of the family, Jesus releases the power of his Holy Spirit.

THE ENTHRONEMENT CELEBRATION

Preparations

1. Obtain a picture or statue of the Sacred Heart. If a priest does not witness the Enthronement, have it blessed in advance.

2. In a prominent place in the living room (or den) prepare a "throne" (fireplace mantel or table) covered with a white cloth and flowers or plants. Place pictures of absent members of the family on this throne.

3. Place the image of the Sacred Heart in another part of the room on another table (or in the dining room). In procession, Jesus will be symbolically escorted to his throne. (By so doing the family re-enacts the triumphal procession of Jesus into Jerusalem on Palm Sunday.) Place candles or vigil lights on this table.

4. Choose a day (if possible) when all the family is present. It is good (but not necessary) to invite some guests, in order to give more glory to Jesus, to acquaint them with the Enthronement, and to allow them to share in the graces of the ceremony. Invite a priest to witness the ceremony. (Note that the presence of the priest, while important, is not strictly necessary.)

5. Prepare for your Enthronement by at least three days of prayer (suggested: the Rosary, at least one decade; New Testament readings: Luke 19:1–10; Luke 10:38–42; Luke 1:26–33; or others). On the day itself (or on the preceding Sunday) the family should make every effort to go to Mass and receive Communion together.

6. Members of the family may compose their own petitions for the "General intercessions".

7. Acquaint yourselves with the meaning of the Enthronement by reading *Enthronement of the Sacred Heart* by Father Larkin. It fully explains the origin, nature and results of Enthronements

in families. Also, it contains the masterful Sacred Heart Encyclical of Pope Piux XII.[4]

8. It is suggested that you design your own "Enthronement Covenant" certificate. An example will be found below.

The Ceremony

1. Read a Scripture passage of your own choice. Reflect and share.

2. The father (or other) reads *"Jesus Speaks to Our Family"*.

JESUS SPEAKS TO OUR FAMILY

"My people, I am your Lord and I rule through my Heart! I desire to be enthroned as Lord of your hearts and of your family as your brother and your friend. I long to share your everyday life, your joys as well as your sorrows.

"My people, whom I love so dearly, behold I stand at the door and knock: if anyone hears my voice and opens the door, I will come in to him and eat with him and he with me (Rev 3:20).

---

[4] National Enthronement Center, Fairhaven, Mass. 02719, or Daughters of St. Paul book stores.

"I am Jesus, your Savior, your liberator. I want to save you and your family from the evil forces working to destroy it, to liberate parents and children from the slavery of sin, the shackles of fear, depression and worry.

"I am ready to release in your home the power of my Spirit, the healer, the consoler, the sanctifier, the teacher.

"But, my people, I will not force my way into your heart or your home. I want to be invited. I am waiting to hear you say to me: *Come Lord Jesus! Stay with us, we need you! Be the Lord, the Brother, the Friend of our family! Send us your Holy Spirit and give us new hearts, a new spirit! Say to us as you did to John: Surely I am coming soon* (Rev 22:20).

"Yes, my people, my Father loves you, I love you, the Holy Spirit loves you—what have you to fear? My wounded heart is the sign and pledge of our merciful love. This heart is open to receive you."

3. After a few moments of silent meditation on Jesus' words, the family gathers around the table before the Sacred Heart image. (If a priest is present he blesses the image.) The father and mother take the Sacred Heart image. Children take the candles and slowly lead the procession

to the throne. A hymn may be sung. ("Jesus is Lord" is appropriate, or "To Jesus Christ Our Sovereign King", or other.)

4. Arriving at the throne, the family gathers in a semi-circle. Before enthroning the Sacred Heart, the father says, **"I now enthrone Jesus as Lord and Friend of our family."** All reply, **"Jesus, we love you, we praise you! We accept your loving rule over our hearts and our family!"** The father now enthrones the Sacred Heart; the children place the candles on either side.

5. All say: **"God is enthroned as King forever!"** (Ps 28) **"All that the Lord has said we will heed and do"** (Ex 24:7).

6. As an act of loving faith in all of Jesus' teachings (manifestations of his love), and as an act of atonement for those who reject or do not practice them, all say *The Apostles' Creed*.

7. Kneeling or standing, the family and guests now say slowly the *Response of the Family*.

RESPONSE OF THE FAMILY

Family Covenant With the Heart of Jesus,
Our Lord and Friend

Jesus, we proclaim you and enthrone you as Lord and Friend of our family! ⋆ **Yes,**

Lord, we do want you to rule over our hearts and wills through your loving heart. ★ Share our everyday life, our joys and sorrows. ★ Be our well-beloved brother, our intimate friend!

Come, Lord Jesus, come! ★ Our hearts and home are open to you. ★ Stay with us, we need you. ★ Release in our home the power of your Spirit, the healer, the consoler. ★ Save our family from the evil forces seeking to destroy us.

Our Father in heaven ★ take away our stony hearts and give us new hearts ★ unselfish, generous, pure hearts, filled with love for you! ★ Heal our hurts, bind up our wounds, unite us in love. ★ May our love go beyond our home ★ and inspire us to love those in need as Jesus loves us.

Lord Jesus, to your loving, glorified Heart, ★ your wounded heart, ★ we dedicate, we consecrate our weak, our selfish hearts. ★ We humbly acknowledge that without you we can do nothing, ★ but with your help and your grace we can do all things: ★ *even though we walk through the valley of the shadow of death, we fear no evil, ★ for you are with us, your rod and your staff, they comfort us.*

Mary, Mother of the Church and our

mother, ★ help us to make our family truly a domestic church ★ that is ★ a community of love, a worshipping, praying family.

Good St. Joseph, head of the Holy Family, ★ watch over us as you watched over Jesus and Mary at Nazareth. ★ Obtain for each of us that same loving trust in divine providence ★ that sustained you in all your trials.

May the Lord bless us and keep us!

May his face shine upon us and be gracious to us!

May he look upon this family with kindness and give us peace!

And may Almighty God bless us, the Father, the Son, and the Holy Spirit. Amen.

Praise the Lord, now and forever. Amen!

8. Prayers for the intention of the Holy Father: Our Father, Hail Mary, Glory be. . . .

9. *General intercessions.* The father (or other) introduces the prayers: **Lord Jesus, You told us, "Whatever you ask the Father in my name, he will give it to you." In your name, and with great confidence, we pray:** *(The response will be:* **Lord, hear our prayer!** *or any other of your choice.)* Members of the family and guests are invited to make their own petitions. Here are a few suggestions:

—For the grace of being faithful to our family covenant. . .

—For an increase of personal, generous love for Jesus. . .

—For greater trust in his merciful love. . .

—That the Holy Spirit may always find our hearts responsive to his call. . .

—For a deeper appreciation of the greatest gift of the Heart of Jesus—the Eucharist— through frequent Mass and Communion and especially on First Fridays or First Saturdays. . .

—That we may receive the sacrament of Penance more often in order to increase our love for Jesus and to avoid sin. . .

—That daily Bible reading and the family Rosary become a part of our family liturgy in our domestic church. . .

—That the Holy Spirit may heal all our hurts and remove from our hearts anything that is preventing us from giving ourselves lovingly to Jesus and to one another. . .

Concluding prayer. **Sacred Heart of Jesus, you promised to bless in a special way those families who honor your divine Heart by enthroning you as Lord and who make a covenant of love with you. Please shower your blessings on this family and all who enter our home. Amen.**

Pope Paul VI urged all families to consecrate themselves to the Immaculate Heart of Mary. An appropriate time would be the First Saturday of the month or on a Feast of Our Lady, particularly the Feast of the Immaculate Heart of Mary, the Saturday following the Solemnity of the Sacred Heart. The following formula may be used.

CONSECRATION TO THE IMMACULATE HEART OF MARY

Queen of the Most Holy Rosary, and tender Mother of the Church ★ we consecrate ourselves to you and to your Immaculate Heart ★ and recommend to your loving care our family ★ families in our neighborhood ★ and families throughout our country.

Please accept our consecration, dearest Mother ★ and use us and all families as you wish ★ to accomplish your designs upon the world. ★ O Spouse of the Holy Spirit, kindle in our hearts and homes the love of purity ★ the practice of a truly Christian family life ★ and the courage to witness to our faith ★ even at the cost of ridicule and suffering.

Make our home a Marian shrine ★ a eucharistic shrine ★ a house of prayer ★ a Christian fortress, a truly domestic church ★ so that through us Jesus may be proclaimed as Lord ★ and loved as a Friend ★ in many

homes in our parish and in our country. Amen.

10. Each member of the family signs the Family Covenant certificate, beginning with the father. Guests may also sign, if desired. The certificate should be framed and hung near the Lord's throne. (See below for sample "covenant".)

11. Conclude with a hymn (optional) and serve refreshments.

12. The Enthronement celebration does not end with the ceremony; that is only the beginning. If Jesus is truly Lord and Friend of your family, try to keep your Enthronement/Covenant alive. Some suggestions: renew your covenant frequently, especially on family anniversaries and First Fridays. At the evening meal encourage a spontaneous renewal especially on the part of the children. And remember to keep your *domestic church* closely linked with the *parish church* by frequent—daily, if possible—Mass and Comunion. Finally, share the good news of your covenant with the Lord with other families, above all those who need healing.

> A beautiful full-color laminated picture of the Sacred Heart, King of Love, Lord of the world, 13 by 16 in., and a companion picture of the Immaculate Heart of Mary, may be obtained

from the National Enthronement Center. Send for the catalogue.

OUR FAMILY COVENANT WITH JESUS THE LORD[5]

Lord Jesus, today_____ 19 ___, we, the members of the _____ family, lovingly enthrone you as Lord and Friend of our family. Freely we make a covenant with you, dedicating to your divine Heart our own hearts and all the members of our family who are not with us. We entrust the fulfillment of our covenant to the Immaculate Heart of your Mother and to Saint Joseph, head of the Holy Family and our protector. We promise to do our best to make our home a domestic church through family prayer and we pledge ourselves to be loyal to the Vicar of Christ and the teachings of the Church.

"All that the Lord has said we will heed and do" (Ex 19:8).

In Token Whereof We Sign

Father	Mother
Children	
Guests	

[5] It is suggested that this "covenant" be hand-lettered by a member of the family, preferably one of the children.